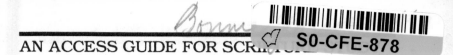
The Gospel According to Mark

Daniel J. Harrington, S.J.

William H. Sadlier, Inc.
New York   Chicago   Los Angeles

Nihil Obstat:
Rev. Msgr. Matthew P. Stapleton
Censor Deputatus

Imprimatur:
✠ Humberto Cardinal Medeiros
Archdiocese of Boston
July 17, 1982

Library of Congress Catalog Card Number: 82-061457
International Standard Book Number: 0-8215-5928-1
123456789/9876543

Published by
William H. Sadlier, Inc.
11 Park Place
New York, New York 10007

Printed and bound in the United States of America

The text of the Gospel of Mark and all other quotations from Scripture are from the *Good News Bible*, the Bible in Today's English Version. Copyright © American Bible Society, 1976.

Contents

"Easy access to sacred Scripture should be provided for all the Christian faithful."

Dogmatic Constitution on Divine Revelation, Vatican II

Preface

The study of Scripture is among the oldest and most traditional religious activities in our Christian heritage. The Gospel of Mark and the Gospel of Luke begin their account of Jesus' public ministry by telling us that he read and preached on the Scriptures in the synagogue in Galilee. It was through their knowledge of the Scriptures that Jesus explained the meaning of his death and resurrection to the two disciples on the way to Emmaus. Readings from the Scriptures have been part of our liturgies since the time of the apostles.

Since the Scriptures are not contemporary works, today's audience needs some guidance to understand fully what the authors are trying to communicate to us about the faith of their communities and the events that generated that great faith. Like most carefully written and thoughtful literature, the books of the Bible have depths of meaning not always apparent to the casual reader. Experience tells us that clear guidance and attentive study can be the key to deeper understanding that will lead to rewarding reflection and prayer.

The *Access Guide* series is designed to help beginning and experienced readers of the sacred Scriptures arrive at a better understanding of the books of the

Bible and a familiarity with their role in the development of faith. Each book has been written by a noted authority on that particular part of the Bible. The language is clear, and the text presented in a highly readable manner.

The general introduction of each study guide acquaints the reader with the background of the particular book of the Bible being studied. It provides information about the biblical author, the historical period in which the book was written, and the nature of the community that was the first audience for the book. The theological themes which summarize the author's message are also discussed, giving the reader an idea of what to look for in considering each section of the book.

A thumbnail sketch of each book of the Bible provides the reader with a basic outline that indicates how the author organized his account of the events in order better to communicate his message. It is interesting to note that, in their original form, the books of the Bible were not divided into chapters and verses. Most had no punctuation or even spaces between the words. The organization of the text, as we know it today, took place at a much later date. Often this organization was done by scholars who failed to appreciate the original organization of the author's thoughts. The sections of the books are organized in these guides in such a way as to reflect the natural internal flow of the original author's manuscripts.

Likewise, since the ancient Hebrew, Greek, and Aramaic languages are no longer commonly spoken, there are many variations in the way the Scriptures are translated into English. The preferred translation for this series is the *Good News Bible* because of its readability in contemporary English. The reader may choose another translation or wish to compare translations which vary. Certainly, recognizing differences in the interpretation of the Scriptures will enhance the reader's ability to get more out of each passage.

The *Access Guide* series is designed for both group and individual study. All the information needed to use the study guides is provided. Groups, however, may wish to have a discussion leader and use the edition of the *Access Guide* which contains notes for the discussion leader. Individual readers and groups participants are encouraged to have a complete Bible on hand for reference purposes.

The material in each study guide is arranged into six study sessions. This format will help those in discussion groups plan each session around a specific sequence of the Scripture text and give some direction to the discussions. A group leader may find it more convenient to rearrange the material into a greater or fewer number of sessions.

Each of the six study sessions contains a portion of Scripture and commentary. Questions for discussion and reflection are meant to lead the reader to probe more deeply into the significance of the Scripture for its first audience and for the contemporary Christian. Naturally, a renewed understanding of the Scriptures and a fresh discovery of the riches contained therein will lead to reflection and prayer and be shared with others through discussion and celebration.

General Introduction to Mark, the First Gospel

The Place of Mark in the New Testament and in the Church

Most New Testament specialists regard Mark as the oldest Gospel. Matthew and Luke apparently used the Gospel of Mark as one of their sources. Since these three Gospels present a "common view" of Jesus as compared with the Gospel of John, they are called the Synoptic Gospels. Mark wrote around A.D. 70. Some fifteen or twenty years later, Matthew and Luke produced independent revisions of Mark and incorporated other early Christian traditions into Mark's story of Jesus.

Mark was a very common name in the Roman world, and the relation between the author of this Gospel and the other persons named Mark in the New Testament (see Acts 12:12, 25; 15:37-39; Colossians 4:10; 2 Timothy 4:11; Philemon 24; 1 Peter 5:13) is not clear. A second-century Christian tradition describes Mark as the interpreter of Peter and thus makes Peter the ultimate authority for this Gospel. But a critical assessment of that tradition raises many problems for historians, and so it is wise to refrain from calling Mark's Gospel "the Gospel of Peter." The evangelist (or "Gospel writer") whom we call Mark had access to early traditions about Jesus and shaped them into a Gospel, but we cannot be sure they came from Peter.

Many of those who had contributed to the recognition of Mark as the earliest Gospel hoped to find in it a strictly factual and nontheological life of Jesus. In this expectation, they were incorrect. Research on Mark during the twentieth century has revealed dramatically the theological character of Mark's interpretation of Jesus. That is not to deny that the Gospel contains facts about Jesus. But it offers much more. The three-year lectionary system instituted in response to the Second Vatican Council has restored Mark to its proper place in the life of the Church, and this Gospel has some very important things to teach us.

The Gospel of Mark should encourage in Christians today a fascination with the person and work of Jesus. In episode after episode, we are led to say: Who is this person? And we learn very quickly not to be satisfied with easy, familiar, or comfortable answers. The wonder-worker and teacher whom we worship as the Son of God suffered a cruel death on the cross. The Gospel also demands that we question where we stand in reference to this Jesus. What does it mean for us to follow a crucified Lord? How do we misunderstand Jesus? Why do we blind ourselves to the rich reality of Christ? How can we improve in our efforts at being Christians?

There are striking similarities between Mark's situation and our own. We too are in a period of cultural upheaval and confusion, and we need to understand and adapt our traditions to respond to changed conditions. We too are being asked difficult questions about our faith, and we need to find in our tradition and in our experience today credible answers. Some Christians are suffering greatly for their faith and, for an increasing number, hostility and persecution are realities. We need to find strength and encouragement in the example of Jesus.

The Purpose of the Writer and the Nature of the Community

The word "gospel" was used by Paul and other early Christians as a way of expressing the importance of Jesus Christ as a guide for living. Jesus is God's own good news. Mark took this word and applied it to his whole account of how God's good news took shape in Jesus of Nazareth. Thus Mark gave new meaning to the term, so that now when it is used, we automatically think of the life of Jesus.

Mark's story of Jesus is not an encyclopedia article about Jesus, nor a scientific biography, nor a theological argument. Rather, it recounts the *decisive encounter* of God with humanity. It does so in the form of a narrative. Written by a believer for believers, Mark's Gospel invites us to enter into the words and actions of the one who is confessed to be the risen Lord present within the Christian community.

What led Mark to write a Gospel? He seems to have written his story of Jesus around A.D. 70. That means that the traditions of Jesus' sayings and deeds had been circulating in oral and written forms for about forty years. One of Mark's purposes was to bring order into these varied traditions and situate them in the life of Jesus. Besides this literary task, Mark was concerned with the fact that more and more non-Jews were becoming Christians. Those people needed instruction about Jesus and about what being a Christian means. His orderly account of Jesus' public activity filled an important need in those circles. The Gospel served as a catechism for catechumens in the early Church.

10

Meanwhile, some difficult questions were being put to Christians. How could Jesus be the Son of God, if he had died a criminal's death on the cross? If Jesus was really the Messiah, why did he not claim this title openly and do what the Messiah was expected to do? What is the relation between the exalted claims being made for Jesus and the Jewish speculations about the end of the world as we know it? What is the relationship between Jesus' followers and the other religious groups among the Jews? Mark found in the traditions about Jesus and in the experience of the early Church the beginnings of answers to these questions. He sought to share them with his readers.

The period around A.D. 70 was not an easy time for a new Jewish religious movement in the Roman empire. The Jews in Palestine had launched a full-scale revolt against the Romans in A.D. 66. The Christian Church would have been perceived by non-Jews as largely Jewish, since Jesus and his first followers were Jews. Furthermore, the newness of this movement aroused hostility from more traditional Jews and suspicion among non-Jews.

Many features in the Gospel of Mark indicate that the evangelist wrote in and for a community that was already suffering persecution or was expecting it very soon. The exact location of the community is not known. It has been traditionally placed at Rome on the basis of the technical Latin words taken over into the Greek text and second-century testimony. Others have argued for Alexandria in Egypt, Antioch in Syria, or Galilee in Palestine. In any case, Mark wished to present the suffering Christ as an example and a source of encouragement to a community living in an atmosphere of hostility and perhaps even persecution.

Literary Patterns

Mark, like the other evangelists, was both a transmitter of tradition and a creative literary artist. He had at his disposal forty years of written and oral materials about Jesus. From careful study of the Gospel, it is possible to identify some of the various forms in which the blocks of tradition were expressed and handed on:

1. Healing stories describe the sick person's condition, the healing activity by Jesus, and the testimony of some third party.

2. Nature miracles tell how Jesus the powerful hero transcends the laws of nature in order to perform helpful actions.

3. Factual narratives transmit information about Jesus or those connected with him. In the time of the Gospel writers, however, history was expected to be related in a way that emphasized the underlying truth of the events.

4. Parables are metaphors or similes drawn from everyday life. They are vivid and somewhat strange, and so they leave the reader's mind in doubt about the precise application.

5. Conflict stories or controversies show how Jesus eluded his opponents' questions and traps by a brilliant saying or action. The result is honor for Jesus and shameful silence for the opponents.

6. Isolated sayings take the forms of proverbs, prophecies, warnings, rules, etc. They express general teachings and appear without much context.

The recognition that Mark had at his disposal these small units of tradition about Jesus should not suggest that he simply put together the pieces in a jigsaw puzzle. In fact, there is evidence that some of these small units had already been joined to form larger blocks of teaching, conflict stories, and miracles. Some connected account of Jesus' passion and death also seems to have been available to the evangelist.

Despite his strong reliance on tradition, Mark demonstrated some literary artistry. First and foremost, he used the traditions about Jesus to develop a geographical and theological plot that traces Jesus' movements from Galilee to Jerusalem. Furthermore, Mark employs frequently and with great success a "sandwich" technique in which he begins a story, interrupts it to tell another story, and then concludes the first story. This device usually highlights some sharp contrast between two characters or groups. Careful attention has been given to the development of the characters of Jesus, the disciples, and other figures.

Major Theological Themes

In his effort at bringing order into the traditions about Jesus, answering the difficult questions being put to Christians, and offering encouragement in the face of persecution, Mark placed special emphasis on Christology (the person and activity of Jesus) and discipleship (the appropriate response to Jesus).

Mark stressed both the human aspect of Jesus and the divine aspect; he never allows one to displace the other. There are hints in the Gospel that some Christians were obsessed with the traditions about Jesus the wonder-worker. In response to such a one-sided interpretation of Jesus, Mark insisted on the extraordinary persuasiveness of Jesus' teaching. But even more important to Mark than Jesus' teaching was the cross.

Everything in the Gospel leads up to, and climaxes in, the story of Jesus' death and resurrection. There is no adequate understanding of Jesus apart from the cross, and his miracles and his teachings can never be separated from his sufferings.

Mark wrote his Gospel on the assumption that there were important similarities between the situation of the first followers of Jesus and the situation of the community in and for which he wrote. Thus what is said about the disciples, has relevance to readers of the Gospel. Early in the story of Jesus, Mark encourages this identification by presenting the disciples in a relatively positive way and by focusing on the problems shared by the disciples and the readers. But, as the inadequacy of the disciples' response to Jesus becomes clear, the readers are forced to put some distance between themselves and the disciples. The increasingly negative example of the disciples demands that the readers seek another way. That way is provided by the example of Jesus.

Within the general context of Christology and discipleship, the hard questions put to the early Christians could be faced and answered. Even though Jesus apparently died a criminal's death, he was innocent of any legal charge and died in accord with God's plan for salvation. Jesus deliberately kept secret the fact that he was the Messiah, lest it be misunderstood in a purely political or this-worldly sense. Jesus' preaching of God's kingdom represented the first step in its coming, and that kingdom will reach its fullness only when Jesus returns as the glorious Son of Man. The movement inspired by Jesus carries with it the wisdom of God and is superior to any other Jewish movement, because its founder surpasses any other Jewish miracle-worker or teacher. The faithful following of Jesus will naturally involve suffering, but persecution does not necessarily mean the defeat of the Christian movement.

A Thumbnail Sketch of Mark

Mark had access to, and made abundant use of, early Christian traditions about Jesus. While remaining faithful to these traditions, he modified them at certain points to bring out their significance for his readers. Above all, he wished to present a full and balanced picture of Jesus.

The evangelist imposed on the blocks of tradition available to him a geographical and theological plan. He tried to show how the miracles and teachings of Jesus recieved a mixed reception in Galilee (1:1—3:6) and how misunderstanding and hostility increased and spread in response to Jesus' ministry there (3:7—6:6). Even Jesus' closest disciples misunderstood him (6:7—8:21) and needed instruction as Jesus and they made their way to Jerusalem (8:22—10:52). In Jerusalem (11:1—13:37) they encountered hostility. All the opposition to, and misunderstanding of, Jesus reach a climax in the story of his passion, death, and resurrection in Jerusalem (14:1—16:8).

Mark's Gospel is sometimes described as a passion narrative with a long introduction. Whatever the merits of that description may be, it does emphasize the decisive importance of the last three chapters of the Gospel. The goal of the geographical-theological outline of the Gospel is the cross in Jerusalem. The opponents' triumph over Jesus is an illusion, for Jesus' true identity as the Son of God is revealed in his death as a "ransom for many" (10:45). Jesus' identity as a wonder-worker and a teacher are balanced by his righteous suffering. Without looking toward the cross, there is no adequate understanding of Jesus.

An outline of the whole Gospel would look something like this:

Part One: Jesus' Authority Is Revealed in Galilee (1:1—3:6)
The prologue (1:1-15); the call of the first disciples (1:16-20) and the eventful day in Capernaum (1:21-45); five conflict stories (2:1—3:6).

Part Two: Jesus Is Rejected in Galilee (3:7—6:6)
Positive and negative responses (3:7-35); parables and explanations (4:1-34); acts of miraculous power (4:35—5:43); the rejection of Jesus by his own people (6:1-6).

Part Three: Jesus Is Misunderstood by His Disciples in Galilee and Beyond (6:7—8:21)
The disciples' mission and John's death (6:7-34); acts of miraculous power and a controversy (6:35—7:23); more acts of miraculous power and a controversy (7:24—8:13); the spiritual blindness of the disciples (8:14-21).

Part Four: Jesus' Instructions to His Disciples on the Way to Jerusalem (8:22—10:52)
The healing of a blind man (8:22-26); three instructions on Christology and discipleship (8:27—9:29; 9:30—10:31; 10:32-45); the healing of a blind man (10:46-52).

Part Five: Jesus' Deeds and Words in Jerusalem (11:1—13:37)
The entrance on the first day (11:1-11); the prophetic teachings on the second day (11:12-19); the explanations (11:20-25), the controversies (11:27-12:44), and the discourse (13:1-37) on the third day.

Part Six: Jesus' Death in Jerusalem (14:1—16:8)
The anointing and the Last Supper (14:1-31); Jesus' prayer and arrest (14:32-52); the trials before the high priest and Pilate (14:53—15:15); the crucifixion and death (15:16-47); the empty tomb (16:1-8); the appendix (16:9-20).

Jesus' Authority
Is Revealed
in Galilee_____ Mark 1:1—3:6

Unlike Matthew and Luke, Mark begins his Gospel with the public ministry of Jesus. He has decided to answer the question: "Who is Jesus?" by immediately telling the story of his words and deeds rather than by first identifying his place in Jewish history and tradition.

Three facts become immediately clear at the beginning of Mark's story about Jesus. 1) Jesus is the Son of God, the Messiah; 2) Jesus has come on a specific mission; 3) his mission is in direct conflict with the world to which he is sent to minister.

Mark begins the Gospel by revealing the secret which Jesus has sought to keep from everyone but his closest disciples. "This is the Good News about Jesus Christ, the Son of God."

As a means of building his case for the identity of Jesus, Mark starts off by clarifying the relationship between John the Baptist and Jesus (1:2-8). The quotations from the Old Testament clearly establish John as the one chosen to prepare others for the coming of the Son of God.

In Mark's time, there were sure to have been those who still followed the preaching of John rather than identifying themselves as followers of Jesus. The evangelist here attempts to resolve any controversy between the two groups by pointing out that, although Jesus was baptized by John, John himself proclaimed Jesus to be the greater, the one who is to come after who will baptize in the Spirit. There is no conflict between the two. It is only after John is arrested that Jesus begins to preach to the same audience.

After clarifying the relation between John the Baptist and Jesus, Mark offers more evidence of Jesus' identity. He is tested by Satan in the wilderness (1:12-13). He overcomes the power of evil, is at one with nature, and is ministered to by angels.

N.B. That Jesus was baptized by John (1:9-11) is certain historically. Indeed it seems to have been a source of embarrassment for some early Christians (see Matthew 3:14-15). The opening of the heavens, the descent of the Holy Spirit, and the heavenly voice indicate the breaking through of the barriers between God and his people through Jesus. The voice identifies Jesus as the Son of God (see Psalm 2:7) and the Servant of God (see Isaiah 42:1).

The good news that was the content of Jesus' preaching is summarized in Mark 1:15. The kingdom of God refers to the establishment and recognition of God's power over all creation. It will take place in a definite way at the end of human history, but this kingship is already begun or inaugurated in the ministry of Jesus.

Mark's Gospel is evidence of the belief among early Christians that the establishment of God's kingdom was imminent. They expected the reign of God to come in their generation, and so there was a sense of urgency about the preaching of the Gospel and the kingdom.

The Gospel According to Mark

1 This is the Good News about Jesus Christ, the Son of God. ²It began as the prophet Isaiah had written:

" 'Here is my messenger,' says God; I will send him ahead of you to open the way for you.'
³"Someone is shouting in the desert:
Get the Lord's road ready for him,
Make a straight path for him to travel!' "

⁴So John appeared in the desert, baptizing people and preaching his message. "Turn away from your sins and be baptized," he told the people, "and God will forgive your sins." ⁵Everybody from the region of Judea and the city of Jerusalem went out to hear John. They confessed their sins and he baptized them in the Jordan river.

⁶John wore clothes made of camel's hair, with a leather belt around his waist; he ate locusts and wild honey. ⁷He announced to the people: "The man who will come after me is much greater than I am; I am not good enough even to bend down and untie his sandals. ⁸I baptize you with water, but he will baptize you with the Holy Spirit."

The Baptism and Temptation of Jesus
(Also Matt. 3.13—4.11; Luke 3.21—22; 4.1—13)

⁹Not long afterward Jesus came from Nazareth, in the region of Galilee, and John baptized him in the Jordan. ¹⁰As soon as Jesus came up out of the water he saw heaven opening and the Spirit coming down on him like a dove. ¹¹And a voice came from heaven: "You are my own dear Son. I am well pleased with you."

¹²At once the Spirit made him go into the desert. ¹³He was there forty days, and Satan tempted him. Wild animals were there also, but angels came and helped him.

Jesus Calls Four Fishermen
(Also Matt. 4.12—22; Luke 4.14—15; 5.1—11)

¹⁴After John had been put in prison, Jesus went to Galilee and preached the Good News from God. ¹⁵"The right time has come," he said, "and the Kingdom of God is near! Turn away from your sins and believe the Good News!"

The Call

This preaching was to be the task of the disciples personally chosen by Jesus to proclaim his message. The first persons summoned to follow Jesus were two pairs of fishermen: Simon and Andrew (1:16-18), and James and John (1:19-20). The Sea of Galilee was the center of a large fishing industry, and the first disciples were businessmen there. There is no reason to consider them illiterate or lacking cleverness, and no reason to assume that they had nothing to lose in following Jesus. Rather, they left behind not only their families but also relatively secure futures in the fishing business.

A very important aspect of discipleship in Mark is being with Jesus, and everything in the call of the first disciples highlights the attractiveness of being with Jesus. The immediate response of those called by Jesus to join him suggests that his character was compelling to those with whom he came in contact.

■ *Reflection*

Would your own impression of Jesus of Nazareth be any different from Mark's description in the Gospel?

[16]As Jesus walked by Lake Galilee, he saw two fishermen, Simon and his brother Andrew, catching fish in the lake with a net. [17]Jesus said to them, "Come with me and I will teach you to catch men." [18]At once they left their nets and went with him.

[19]He went a little further on and saw two other brothers, James and John, the sons of Zebedee. They were in their boat getting their nets ready. [20]As soon as Jesus saw them he called them; so they left their father Zebedee in the boat with the hired men and went with Jesus.

The Eventful Day

Jesus' first public action in 1:21-28 presents him as a teacher and as a miracle-worker. Capernaum was the geographical center of much of Jesus' ministry in Galilee. At the synagogue there Jesus is invited to speak, as anyone with sufficient wisdom might be. His authority to teach is underscored by the dramatic cure of one possessed by an evil spirit.

This eventful day in Capernaum also includes the healing of Simon Peter's mother-in-law (1:29-31). In this case Jesus shows his power over a fever. With his summary in 1:32-34, Mark indicates that Jesus performed more miracles than are narrated in the Gospel. The exorcism in 1:23-27 and the healing in 1:29-31 are only samples. In the Bible, miracles are signs that God is at work. Unexpected recoveries from illness, reversals in battle, sudden storms and other extraordinary occurrences are classed as miracles. In these cases, Jesus' power is at work, a clear indication of his power to teach. Mark also stresses Jesus' absolute mastery of physical and spiritual life. The teachings and the miracles are a sign of the new order of God's kingdom.

The final miracle of chapter 1, the cure of the leper, ushers in the theme of the controversy with the religious leadership of the time. The "leper" healed by Jesus in 1:40-45 suffered from a skin disease that disqualified him from being part of the community. In order to bring about reunion with the community, Jesus instructs the healed leper to observe the rules laid down in Leviticus 14. Jesus seems to be very willing to cooperate with the Mosaic law and with those whose responsibility it was to teach and administer it.

■ *Reflection*

Are there miracles performed in our time? If so, by whom and how can we recognize a miraculous event?

A Man with an Evil Spirit
(Also Luke 4.31–37)

[21]They came to the town of Capernaum, and on the next Sabbath day Jesus went into the synagogue and began to teach. [22]The people who heard him were amazed at the way he taught. He wasn't like the teachers of the Law; instead, he taught with authority.

²³Just then a man with an evil spirit in him came into the synagogue and screamed: ²⁴"What do you want with us, Jesus of Nazareth? Are you here to destroy us? I know who you are: you are God's holy messenger!" ²⁵Jesus commanded the spirit: "Be quiet, and come out of the man!" ²⁶The evil spirit shook the man hard, gave a loud scream and came out of him. ²⁷The people were all so amazed that they started saying to each other, "What is this? Some kind of new teaching? This man has authority to give orders to the evil spirits, and they obey him!" ²⁸And so the news about Jesus spread quickly everywhere in the region of Galilee.

²⁹They left the synagogue and went straight to the home of Simon and Andrew; and James and John went with them. ³⁰Simon's mother-in-law was sick in bed with a fever, and as soon as Jesus got there he was told about her. ³¹He went to her, took her by the hand and helped her up. The fever left her and she began to wait on them.

³²When evening came, after the sun had set, people brought to Jesus all the sick and those who had demons. ³³All the people of the town gathered in front of the house. ³⁴Jesus healed many who were sick with all kinds of diseases and drove out many demons. He would not let the demons say anything, because they knew who he was.

Jesus Preaches in Galilee
(Also Luke 4.42–44)

³⁵Very early the next morning, long before daylight, Jesus got up and left the house. He went out of town to a lonely place where he

prayed. [36]But Simon and his companions went out searching for him; [37]when they found him they said, "Everyone is looking for you." [38]But Jesus answered: "We must go on to the other villages around here. I have to preach to them also, because that is why I came." [39]So he traveled all over Galilee, preaching in the synagogues and driving out demons.

Jesus Heals a Man
(Also Matt. 8.1—4; Luke 5.12—16)

[40]A leper came to Jesus, knelt down, and begged him for help. "If you want to," he said, "you can make me clean." [41]Jesus was filled with pity and reached out and touched him. "I do want to," he answered. "Be clean!" [42]At once the leprosy left the man and he was clean. [43]Then Jesus spoke harshly with him and sent him away at once. [44]"Listen," he said, "don't tell this to anyone, But go straight to the priest and let him examine you: then offer the sacrifice that Moses ordered, to prove to everyone that you are now clean." [45]But the man went away and began to spread the news everywhere. Indeed, he talked so much that Jesus could not go into a town publicly. Instead he stayed out in lonely places, and people came to him from everywhere.

Conflicts and Challenges

The story of the eventful day is followed by five conflict stories or controversies in 2:1—3:6. The five passages involve issues that would have been matters of debate between the early Christians in Palestine and the members of the Jewish synagogues, and so they provided precedents based on the example of Jesus himself for dealing with these matters. The five stories also introduce the scribes, the Pharisees, and the Herodians, the opponents of Jesus. Here Jesus outdoes his opponents in debate, but his superiority sets the stage for their more active hostility later in the Gospel.

The first conflict (2:1-12) involves Jesus' power to forgive sins. The story of the healing of the paralyzed man is sandwiched around the debate about the power to forgive sins. Mark's vivid dramatization of the story involves the reader in the surprise of the witnesses in the house. Jesus does the unexpected to make a point about his full purpose and mission. Jesus asserts himself as being more than just another preacher and healer. He has the power of spiritual healing as well, a power understood to belong only to God.

The second conflict (2:13-17) involves the kind of people with whom Jesus associated. First we hear about Levi the tax collector. Tax collectors were never popular, but they were especially suspect among Jews of Jesus' time because their profession demanded contact with non-Jews, and because some tax collectors were dishonest. The fact that Jesus invited someone with this occupation to be his disciple scandalized his opponents.

Another source of amazement was Jesus' practice of eating with tax collectors and sinners. The Pharisees looked on their common meals as religious occasions and dined only with people who observed the Old Testament laws of ritual purity. The people described as sinners in 2:15 either had bad reputations or belonged to social classes that paid no attention to the laws of purity. For Jesus to eat with such suspicious characters indicated to the Pharisees that he was not a seriously religious person.

The third and central conflict (2:18-22) concerns fasting. The Old Testament says little about fasting, and encourages it primarily on the Day of Atonement. But pious people like the Pharisees and the disciples of John the Baptist fasted more often. Since Jesus was getting a reputation as a religious leader, people would naturally expect him and his disciples to fast also, but Jesus' disciples did not practice frequent fasts.

The fourth conflict takes its rise from the disciples' actions as they and Jesus make their way through the grain fields on the Sabbath (2:23-28). The Sabbath began at sunset on Friday and ended at sunset on Saturday. It was a time for prayer and rest, and no work was to be done in it. But Jesus defends his disciples on the grounds that he is the Lord of the Sabbath.

The fifth and final controversy (3:1-6) concerns the issue of work on the Sabbath. Once more the teaching section is sandwiched in between the account of a healing. Once again the healing takes place in the synagogue, the center for religious teaching, where Jesus first preached and manifested this power of healing. The conflicts end with the report about Jesus' enemies joining forces to kill him.

■ *Reflection*

In our Church today, are there any religious groups or parties which disagree substantially with one another?

Jesus Heals a Paralyzed Man
(Also Matt. 9.1—8; Luke 5.17—26)

2 A few days later Jesus came back to Capernaum, and the news spread that he was at home. ²So many people came together that there wasn't any room left, not even out in front of the door. Jesus was preaching the

message to them ³when some people came, bringing him a paralyzed man—four of them were carrying him. ⁴Because of the crowd, however, they could not get him to Jesus. So they made a hole in the roof right above the place where Jesus was. When they had made an opening, they let the man down, lying on his mat. ⁵Jesus saw how much faith they had, and said to the paralyzed man, "My son, your sins are forgiven."

⁶Some teachers of the Law who were sitting there thought to themselves: ⁷"How does he dare to talk against God like this? No man can forgive sins; only God can!" ⁸At once Jesus knew their secret thoughts, so he said to them: "Why do you think such things? ⁹Is it easier to say to this paralyzed man, 'Your sins are forgiven,' or to say, 'Get up, pick up your mat, and walk'? ¹⁰I will prove to you, then, that the Son of Man has authority on earth to forgive sins." So he said to the paralyzed man, ¹¹"I tell you, get up, pick up your mat, and go home!" ¹²While they all watched, the man got up, picked up his mat and hurried away. They were all completely amazed and praised God, saying, "We have never seen anything like this!"

Jesus Calls Levi
(Also Matt. 9.9–13; Luke 5.27–32)

¹³Jesus went back again to the shore of Lake Galilee. A crowd came to him and he started teaching them. ¹⁴As he walked along he saw a tax collector, Levi the son of Alphaeus, sitting in his office. Jesus said to him, "Follow me." Levi got up and followed him.

¹⁵Later on Jesus was having a meal in Levi's house. There were many tax collectors and outcasts who were following Jesus, and some of them joined him and his disciples at the table. ¹⁶Some teachers of the Law, who were Pharisees, saw that Jesus was eating with these outcasts and tax collectors; so they asked his disciples, "Why does he eat with tax collectors and outcasts?" ¹⁷Jesus heard them and answered: "People who are well do not need a doctor, but only those who are sick. I have not come to call the respectable people, but the outcasts."

The Question About Fasting
(Also Matt. 9.14–17; Luke 5.33–39)

¹⁸On one occasion the followers of John the Baptist and the Pharisees were fasting. Some people came to Jesus and asked him, "Why is it that the disciples of John the Baptist and the disciples of the Pharisees fast, but yours do not?" ¹⁹Jesus answered: "Do you expect the guests at a wedding party to go without food? Of course not! As long as the bridegroom is with them they will not do that. ²⁰But the time will come when the bridegroom will be taken away from them; when that day comes then they will go without food.

²¹"No one uses a piece of new cloth to patch up an old coat. If he does, the new patch will tear off some of the old cloth, making an even bigger hole. ²²Nor does anyone pour new wine into used wineskins. If he does, the wine will burst the skins, and both the wine and the skins will be ruined. No! Fresh skins for new wine!"

²³Jesus was walking through some wheat fields on a Sabbath day. As his disciples walked along with him, they began to pick the heads of wheat. ²⁴So the Pharisees said to Jesus, "Look, it is against our Law for your disciples to do this on the Sabbath!" ²⁵Jesus answered: "Have you never read what David did that time when he needed something to eat? He and his men were hungry, ²⁶so he went into the house of God and ate the bread offered to God. This happened when Abiathar was the High Priest. According to our Law only the priests may eat this bread—but David ate it, and even gave it to his men." ²⁷And Jesus said, "The Sabbath was made for the good of man; man was not made for the Sabbath. ²⁸So the Son of Man is Lord even of the Sabbath."

The Man with a Paralyzed Hand
(Also Matt. 12.9—14; Luke 6.6—11)

3 Then Jesus went back to the synagogue, where there was a man who had a crippled hand. ²Some people were there who wanted to accuse Jesus of doing wrong; so they watched him very closely, to see whether he would cure anyone on the Sabbath. ³Jesus said to the man with the crippled hand, "Come up here to the front." ⁴Then he asked the people: "What does our Law allow us to do on the Sabbath? To help, or to harm? To save a man's life, or to destroy it?" But they did not say a thing. ⁵Jesus was angry as he looked around at them, but at the same time he felt sorry for them, because they were so stubborn and wrong. Then he said to the man, "Stretch out your hand." He stretched it out and it became well again. ⁶So the Pharisees left the meeting house and

met at once with some members of Herod's party; and they made plans against Jesus to kill him.

■ Discussion

1. In what ways does Mark show that Jesus is the Son of God?
2. Can you think of any reason why Jesus might wish to keep his identity a secret?
3. How does Mark describe Jesus' mission? In what passages does Jesus explain himself?
4. Why do you think Mark has combined teaching stories with healing stories?
5. What reasons did the various religious groups have for rejecting Jesus and his teaching?
6. What insights into Jesus' person do you see coming through Mark's account of these events? Why would such a person be so attractive to the first disciples?

■ Prayer and Meditation

"In days to come
    the mountain where the Temple stands
    will be the highest one of all,
    towering above all the hills.
Many nations will come streaming to it,
    and their people will say,
'Let us go up the hill of the LORD.
    to the Temple of Israel's God.
He will teach us what he wants us to do;
    we will walk in the paths he has chosen.
For the LORD'S teaching comes for Jerusalem;
    from Zion he speaks to his people.'
Now, descendants of Jacob, let us walk in the light
    which the LORD gives us!' ''

Isaiah 2: 2,3,5

Jesus Is Rejected in Galilee —————— Mark 3:7—6:6

Mark 3:7-12 serves as a bridge between the first major section of the Gospel in which Jesus' great powers are made manifest and the second section (3:13—6:6) in which there is a growing opposition to him. The language, style, and content of this transitional report indicate that it was composed by Mark himself and was not a traditional piece taken over by him.

Mark seems to imply that the crowds are attracted to Jesus because of the miracles he has performed. The crowds by this time are no longer just the local people. The entire region of Palestine is represented. The crowds were so great and enthusiastic that Jesus had a boat ready to avoid being crushed.

A Crowd by the Lake

⁷Jesus and his disciples went away to Lake Galilee, and a large crowd followed him. They came from Galilee, from Judea, ⁸from Jerusalem, from the territory of Idumea, from the territory on the other side of the Jordan, and from the neighborhood of the cities of Tyre and Sidon. This large crowd came to Jesus because they heard of the things he was doing. ⁹The crowd was so large that Jesus told his disciples

to get a boat ready for him, so the people would not crush him. ¹⁰He had healed many people, and all the sick kept pushing their way to him in order to touch him. ¹¹And whenever the people who had evil spirits in them saw him they would fall down before him and scream, "You are the Son of God!" ¹²Jesus gave a stern command to the evil spirits not to tell who he was.

Names

Mark continues the theme of keeping Jesus' identity a secret. Actually, there are several examples in this section of the Gospel which illustrate the double meanings of names. For the people of Jesus' time to know another's name was not only to perceive his or her identity, but to hold some power over that person. Jesus forbids the unclean spirit to speak his name both to keep secret his true identity and to prohibit the evil spirit from having any power over him.

Jesus highlights the importance of the personal name by giving Simon the name Peter and giving James and John a second name as brothers. These were not understood as nicknames, but rather as new identities and signs that these men belonged to Jesus in a unique way.

The Calling of the Twelve

Up to this time, Jesus had called the four fishermen and Levi the tax collector to be his disciples. Now in 3:13-19 he fixes at twelve the number of disciples that will be with him until his death in Jerusalem.

The choice of the twelve takes place in the mountains. Mark's mention of the location of the choosing of the apostles may be his way of adding special significance to the event. Moses received the tablets of the law on a mountain, and the number of apostles corresponds to the number of tribes of Israel. Whereas this may seem incidental to the modern reader, it could associate for Mark's contemporaries in the Jewish community with a continuity of the mission of Israel.

The task of the twelve disciples is to preach the good news. They are also given authority to cast out demons. This, of course, relates to two of the principal activities of Jesus' ministry.

Jesus Chooses the Twelve Apostles
(Also Matt. 10.1–4; Luke 6.12–16)

¹³Then Jesus went up a hill and called to himself the men he wanted. They came to him ¹⁴and he chose twelve, whom he named apostles. "I have chosen you to stay with me," he told them; "I will also send you out to preach, ¹⁵and you will have authority to drive out demons." ¹⁶These are the twelve he chose: Simon (Jesus gave him the name Peter); ¹⁷James and his brother John, the sons of Zebedee (Jesus gave them the name Boanerges, which means "Men of Thunder"); ¹⁸Andrew, Philip, Bartholomew, Matthew, Thomas, James the son of Alphaeus, Thaddaeus, Simon the patriot, ¹⁹and Judas Iscariot, who became the traitor.

Jesus Defends His Actions

In contrast to the enthusiasm of the crowds and the twelve disciples, two groups in 3:20-35 make very negative judgments about Jesus. The first negative judgment on Jesus is made in 3:21 by "those around him," probably his relatives and friends in Galilee. The second negative judgment about Jesus is made in 3:22 by the scribes who were intellectuals skilled in interpreting and applying the laws of the Old Testament to the problems of everyday life.

In 3:23-30 Jesus responds to the negative judgment made by the scribes. His method is to use parables, which are brief and picturesque stories designed to make the point indirectly. Note that the scribes admit the remarkable character of Jesus' activity. They assume that it was so extraordinary as to need some super-human force behind it. The question at issue is the source of Jesus' power, not the fact of it.

Having exposed the foolishness of the scribes' assessment of him in 3:23-27, Jesus offers a comment on the seriousness of their erroneous judgment in 3:28-30. Every sin can be forgiven except blasphemy against the Holy Spirit, which is the refusal to recognize the Spirit as the power behind Jesus.

In 3:31-35 Jesus responds to the negative judgment made by "those around him," probably his relatives and friends in Galilee. The term "brothers" had a wide range of meaning in Palestine, and does not necessarily refer to other children born of Mary. Jesus' response redefines his family as those who seek and do God's will.

Jesus and Beelzebul
(Also Matt. 12.22–32; Luke 11.14–23; 12.10)

²⁰Then Jesus went home. Again such a large crowd gathered that Jesus and his disciples had no time to eat. ²¹When his family heard about this they set out to get him, because people were saying, "He's gone mad!"

²²Some teachers of the Law who had come from Jerusalem were saying, "He has Beelzebul in him!" Others said, "It is the chief of

the demons who gives him the power to drive them out." ²³So Jesus called the people to him and told them some parables: "How can Satan drive out Satan? ²⁴If a country divides itself into groups that fight each other, that country will fall apart. ²⁵If a family divides itself into groups that fight each other, that family will fall apart. ²⁶So if Satan's kingdom divides into groups, it cannot last, but will fall apart and come to an end.

²⁷"No one can break into a strong man's house and take away his belongings unless he ties up the strong man first; then he can plunder his house.

²⁸"Remember this! Men can be forgiven all their sins and all the evil things they say, no matter how often they say them. ²⁹But the person who says evil things against the Holy Spirit can never be forgiven, for he has committed an eternal sin." ³⁰(Jesus said this because some had said, "He has an evil spirit in him.")

Jesus' Mother and Brothers
(Also Matt. 12.46–50; Luke 8.19–21)

³¹Then Jesus' mother and brothers arrived. They stood outside the house and sent in a message, asking for him. ³²A crowd was sitting around Jesus, and they told him, "Look, your mother and brothers are outside, and they want you." ³³Jesus answered, "Who is my mother? Who are my brothers?" ³⁴He looked over the people sitting around him and said, "Look! Here are my mother and my brothers! ³⁵For the person who does what God wants him to do is my brother, my sister, my mother."

Parables of the Kingdom

Mark 4:1-34 consists of parables and explanations. One of the purposes of this passage is to comment on the mixed reception given to Jesus in 3:7-35. Another important purpose is to give some idea about the coming of God's kingdom, its dimensions, and its timing. The passage expands on the summary of Jesus' preaching in 1:15: " 'The right time has come,' he said, 'and the Kingdom of God is near! Turn away from your sins and believe the Good News!' "

■ Reflection

Are there any contemporary pieces of literature or film that might qualify as "parables of the kingdom"?

The Sower

The first parable (4:3-9) is traditionally called the parable of the sower. It takes as its background the way in which seeds were planted in Palestine in Jesus' time. If we identify Jesus as the sower and his preaching of the kingdom (see 1:15) as the seed, we can see the parable as a comment on the reception of Jesus' preaching by various groups among his audience. There is nothing lacking in either the sower or the seed, only in the condition of some of the soil on which it fell. The good soil, however, yields a remarkable harvest.

An explanation of the mysterious and elusive character of Jesus' parables is supplied in 4:10-12. The parables demand reflection and interpretation if their precise application is ever to be grasped. It is clear that neither the crowds nor the disciples immediately understood the meaning of the parables.

Jesus' explanation of the parable of the sower can be applied on two levels. Certainly he is referring to those to whom he spoke the parable in person. Some with little faith or depth will criticize his teaching or his work; others will accept Jesus and share in his mission.

The second level is Mark's audience, the Christian community in the midst of conflict and persecution. Only those properly disposed (the good soil) will accept the Gospel and bear fruit as Christians.

After the interpretation of the parable, Jesus returns in 4:21-25 to the apparent obscurity of the parables. The first part (4:21-23) compares Jesus' preaching to a lamp, and the second part (4:24-25) describes the response to Jesus' preaching.

■ Reflection

According to the parable of the sower, what kind of "soil" would characterize our receptiveness to the Word of God?

The Parable of the Sower
(Also Matt. 13.1–9; Luke 8.4–8)

4 Again Jesus began to teach by Lake Galilee. The crowd that gathered around him was so large that he got into a boat and sat in it. The boat was out in the water, while the crowd stood on the shore, at the water's edge. ²He used parables to teach them many things, and in his teaching said to them: ³"Listen! There was a man who went out to sow. ⁴As he scattered the seed in the field, some of it fell along the path, and the birds came and ate it up. ⁵Some of it fell on rocky ground, where there was little soil. The seeds soon sprouted, because the soil wasn't deep. ⁶Then when the sun came up it burned the young plants, and because the roots had not grown deep enough the plants soon dried up. ⁷Some of

the seed fell among thorns, which grew up and choked the plants, and they didn't bear grain. ⁸But some seeds fell in good soil, and the plants sprouted, grew, and bore grain: some had thirty grains, others sixty, and others one hundred." ⁹And Jesus said, "Listen, then, if you have ears to hear with!"

The Purpose of the Parables
(Also Matt. 13.10–17; Luke 8.9–10)

¹⁰When Jesus was alone, some of those who had heard him came to him with the twelve disciples and asked him to explain the parables. ¹¹"You have been given the secret of the Kingdom of God," Jesus answered; "but the others, who are on the outside, hear all things by means of parables, ¹²so that,

'They may look and look, yet not see,
They may listen and listen, yet not understand,
For if they did, they might turn to God
And he would forgive them.' "

Jesus Explains the Parable of the Sower
(Also Matt. 13.18–23; Luke 8.11–15)

¹³Then Jesus asked them: "Don't you understand this parable? How, then, will you ever understand any parable? ¹⁴The sower sows God's message. ¹⁵Sometimes the message falls along the path; these people hear it, but as soon as they hear it Satan comes and takes away the message sown in them. ¹⁶Other people are like the seeds that fall on rocky ground. As soon as they hear the message they receive it gladly. ¹⁷But it does not sink deep into them,

and they don't last long. So when trouble or persecution comes because of the message, they give up at once. [18]Other people are like the seeds sown among the thorns. These are the ones who hear the message, [19]but the worries about this life, the love for riches, and all other kinds of desires crowd in and choke the message, and they don't bear fruit. [20]But other people are like the seeds sown in good soil. They hear the message, accept it, and bear fruit: some thirty, some sixty, and some one hundred."

A Lamp Under a Bowl
(Also Luke 8.16—18)

[21]And Jesus continued: "Does anyone ever bring in a lamp and put it under a bowl or under the bed? Doesn't he put it on the lampstand? [22]Whatever is hidden away will be brought out into the open, and whatever is covered up will be uncovered. [23]Listen, then, if you have ears to hear with!"

[24]He also said to them: "Pay attention to what you hear! The same rules you use to judge others will be used by God to judge you—and with even greater severity. [25]The man who has something will be given more; the man who has nothing will have taken away from him even the little he has."

The Kingdom

By means of another seed parable (4:26-29), Jesus teaches about the coming of God's kingdom. Its coming is like what happens when a farmer sows seed and waits patiently for the harvest. The center of attention of this parable is the seed. It grows without the farmer's assistance or understanding. Once the Word is preached, the kingdom will grow.

A third parable, that of the mustard seed, is used in 4:30-32 to illustrate the coming of God's kingdom. In each of the parables in this section, Jesus compares the preaching of the Word to the sowing or planting of seed of various kinds. The growth that results from that planting is likened to the establishment and growth of God's kingdom. In each case, the flourishing of the kingdom has a miraculous quality about it: the extraordinary yield of grain, the mystery of growth, the tiny mustard seed which becomes the biggest of all plants.

The Parable of the Growing Seed

[26]Jesus went on to say: "The Kingdom of God is like a man who scatters seed in his field. [27]He sleeps at night, is up and about during the day, and all the while the seeds are sprouting and growing. Yet he does not know how it happens. [28]The soil itself makes the plants grow and bear fruit: first the tender stalk appears, then the head, and finally the head full of grain. [29]When the grain is ripe the man starts working with his sickle, for harvest time has come."

The Parable of the Mustard Seed
(Also Matt. 13.31–32, 34; Luke 13.18–19)

[30]"What shall we say the Kingdom of God is like?" asked Jesus. "What parable shall we use to explain it? [31]It is like a mustard seed, the smallest seed in the world. A man takes it and plants it in the ground; [32]after a while it grows

up and becomes the biggest of all plants. It puts out such large branches that the birds come and make their nests in its shade."

[33]Jesus preached his message to the people, using many other parables like these; he told them as much as they could understand. [34]He would not speak to them without using parables; but when he was alone with his disciples he would explain everything to them.

Jesus Calms the Storm and Expels Demons

The teaching in parables is followed by more acts of miraculous power done by Jesus: the calming of the storm (4:35-41), the healing of the possessed man (5:1-20), and healings of the daughter of Jairus and the woman with severe bleeding (5:21-43). This part of the Gospel climaxes in the rejection of Jesus in his own home area (6:1-6). Once more the good and powerful wonder-worker encounters some negative reactions.

The first act of power is the stilling of the storm. Jesus is here setting out in a new direction to the other side of Lake Galilee. A great wind storm arises and threatens to overwhelm the boat with Jesus and his disciples in it. Using the same words that he used to cast out the unclean spirit in 1:25, Jesus calms the wind and the sea. This may indicate that Mark views both events as evidence of Jesus's power in the cosmic struggle between good and evil.

The second act of power done by Jesus is an exorcism or expulsion of a demon (5:1-20). Having travelled to the other side of the Sea of Galilee, Jesus and the disciples arrive in the country of the Gerasenes. But the city of Gerasa was thirty miles from the shore. According to Matthew, the incident took place in the territory of the Gadarenes. The city of Gadara was much closer to the shore. This geographical problem should not detract from the fact that here for the first time Jesus has left Galilee and entered non-Jewish territory.

The exorcism itself is presented in 5:9-13. In the encounter, possessing the opponent's name is a way of gaining power. The demon knows Jesus' name, and Jesus discovers the demon's name. But the power struggle is uneven. The demon has no hope of triumphing over Jesus.

After the exorcism, the healed man requests that he be allowed to go with Jesus as his disciple. Jesus denies this request, but instructs him to proclaim what the Lord has done. In light of the other healing stories in Mark, this request is surprising. Jesus does not instruct the man to keep silent. Perhaps it is no coincidence that this man is a gentile, and all the others healed to this point belonged to the Jewish community.

Jesus Calms a Storm
(Also Matt. 8.23–27; Luke 8.22–25)

[35]On the evening of that same day Jesus said to his disciples, "Let us go across to the other side of the lake." [36]So they left the crowd; the disciples got into the boat that Jesus was already in, and took him with them. Other boats were there too. [37]A very strong wind blew up and the waves began to spill over into the boat, so that it was about to fill with water. [38]Jesus was in the back of the boat, sleeping with his head on a pillow. The disciples woke him up and said, "Teacher, don't you care that we are about to die?" [39]Jesus got up and commanded the wind: "Be quiet!" and said to the waves, "Be still!" The wind died down, and there was a great calm. [40]Then Jesus said to

them, "Why are you frightened? Are you still without faith?" ⁴¹But they were terribly afraid, and began to say to each other, "Who is this man? Even the wind and the waves obey him!"

Jesus Heals a Man with Evil Spirits
(Also Matt.8.28–34; Luke 8.26–39)

5 So they came to the other side of Lake Galilee, to the territory of the Gerasenes. ²As soon as Jesus got out of the boat he was met by a man who came out of the burial caves. ³This man had an evil spirit in him and lived among the graves. Nobody could keep him tied with chains any more; ⁴many times his feet and hand had been tied, but every time he broke the chains, and smashed the irons on his feet. He was too strong for anyone to stop him! ⁵Day and night he wandered among the graves and through the hills, screaming and cutting himself with stones.

⁶He was some distance away when he saw Jesus; so he ran, fell on his knees before him, ⁷and screamed in a loud voice, "Jesus, Son of the Most High God! What do you want with me? For God's sake, I beg you, don't punish me!" (⁸He said this because Jesus was saying to him, "Evil spirit, come out of this man!")

⁹So Jesus asked him, "What is your name?" The man answered, "My name is 'Mob'—there are so many of us!" ¹⁰And he kept begging Jesus not to send the evil spirits out of that territory.

¹¹A large herd of pigs was nearby, feeding on the hillside. ¹²The spirits begged Jesus, "Send us to the pigs, and let us go into them." ¹³So he let them. The evil spirits went out of the

man and went into the pigs. The whole herd—about two thousand pigs in all—rushed down the side of the cliff into the lake and were drowned.

¹⁴The men who had been taking care of the pigs ran away and spread the news in the town and among the farms. The people went out to see what had happened. ¹⁵They came to Jesus and saw the man who used to have the mob of demons in him; he was sitting there, clothed and in his right mind—and they were all afraid. ¹⁶Those who had seen it told the people what had happened to the man with the demons, and about the pigs. ¹⁷So they began to ask Jesus to leave their territory.

¹⁸As Jesus was getting into the boat, the man who had had the demons begged him, "Let me go with you!" ¹⁹But Jesus would not let him. Instead he told him, "Go back home to your family and tell them how much the Lord has done for you, and how kind he has been to you!" ²⁰So the man left and went all through the Ten Towns telling what Jesus had done for him; and all who heard it were filled with wonder.

Healing the Sick and Raising the Dead

Having demonstrated Jesus' power over the sea and the demons, Mark presents in 5:21-43 two stories showing Jesus as victorious over physical sickness and even over death. The two stories appear in the sandwich format. This format appeared earlier in the healing of the paralytic (2:1-12) where a discussion of Jesus' power to forgive sins was "sandwiched" in with the story of the miraculous cure.

Here the issue is Jesus' power over physical evil. The implication is that those who have faith are the recipients of this power in that the woman who was cured was the only one touching Jesus who received the benefit of this power.

In the case of the healing and the raising of Jairus' daughter to life (5:21-23, 35-43), the terms used—faith, make well, arise, get up, peace—were all part of the early Church's vocabulary of spiritual salvation. The use of these terms points to Jesus' resurrection and its power to give others eternal life. The mourners who make fun of Jesus' statement that the girl is not dead do not understand the identity of the man in their midst. "Don't be afraid, only believe," are the words of Jesus that Mark uses to address his own contemporaries whose faith in the resurrection may waver. The secret is once more made manifest: Jesus is the Son of God.

Jairus' Daughter and the Woman Who Touched Jesus' Cloak
(Also Matt. 9.18–26; Luke 8.40–56)

[21]Jesus went back across to the other side of the lake. There at the lakeside a large crowd gathered around him. [22]Jairus, an official of the local synagogue, came up, and when he saw Jesus he threw himself down at his feet [23]and begged him as hard as he could: "My little daughter is very sick. Please come and place your hands on her, so that she will get well and live!" [24]Then Jesus started off with him. So many people were going along with him that they were crowding him from every side.

[25]There was a woman who had suffered terribly from severe bleeding for twelve years, [26]even though she had been treated by many doctors. She had spent all her money, but in-

stead of getting better she got worse all the time. ²⁷She had heard about Jesus, so she came in the crowd behind him. ²⁸"If I touch just his clothes," she said to herself, "I shall get well." ²⁹She touched his cloak and her bleeding stopped at once; and she had the feeling inside herself that she was cured of her trouble. ³⁰At once Jesus felt that power had gone out of him. So he turned around in the crowd and said, "Who touched my clothes?"

³¹His disciples answered, "You see that the people are crowding you; why do you ask who touched you?" ³²But Jesus kept looking around to see who had done it. ³³The woman realized what had happened to her; so she came, trembling with fear, and fell at his feet and told him the whole truth. ³⁴Jesus said to her, "My daughter, your faith has made you well. Go in peace, and be healed from your trouble."

³⁵While Jesus was saying this, some messengers came from Jairus' house and told him, "Your daughter has died. Why should you bother the Teacher any longer? ³⁶Jesus paid no attention to what they said, but told him, "Don't be afraid, only believe." ³⁷Then he did not let anyone go on with him except Peter and James and his brother John. ³⁸They arrived at the official's house, where Jesus saw the confusion and heard all the loud crying and wailing. ³⁹He went in and said to them, "Why all this confusion? Why are you crying? The child is not dead—she is only sleeping!" ⁴⁰They all started making fun of him, so he put them all out, took the child's father and mother, and his three disciples and went into the room where the child was lying. ⁴¹He took her by the hand and said to her, *Talitha koum*, which means, "Little girl! Get up, I tell you!" ⁴²She got up at once and started walking around. (She was

twelve years old.) When this happened they were completely amazed! ⁴³But Jesus gave them strict orders not to tell anyone, and said, "Give her something to eat."

Nazareth

In 6:1-6 Jesus returns to Nazareth in Galilee. He has shown himself master over the sea, the demons, illness, and even death. In his struggle against the forces of evil, he has been victorious. But he had not convinced everyone in Galilee. Far from it! Even those who should have known him best rejected him. Thus he suffers the prophet's fate, and performs few miracles there because of the people's lack of faith.

Jesus Is Rejected at Nazareth
(Also Matt. 13.53–58; Luke 4.16–30)

6 Jesus left that place and went back to his home town, followed by his disciples. ²On the Sabbath day he began to teach in the synagogue. Many people were there, and when they heard him they were all amazed. "Where did he get all this?" they asked. "What wisdom is this that has been given him? How does he perform miracles? ³Isn't he the carpenter, the son of Mary, and the brother of James, Joseph, Judas, and Simon? Aren't his sisters living here?" And so they rejected him. ⁴Jesus said to them: "A prophet is respected everywhere except in his home town, and by his relatives and his family." ⁵He wasn't able to perform any miracles there, except that he placed his hands on a few sick people and healed them. ⁶He was greatly surprised, because they did not have faith.

■ Reflection

Does our own Christian community show signs that as a group we understand Jesus' preaching and the meaning of the parables?

■ Discussion

1. What are some central themes of the parables in Mark's Gospel?
2. What do you think is the key element in being able to understand the meaning of the parables?
3. What are the forces of evil that Jesus encounters in Mark's account?
4. What have we learned about the person of Jesus through these encounters with those who reject him?
5. Is there a clear-cut lesson for the disciples of Christ that can be learned by reading this section of Mark's Gospel?

■ Prayer and Meditation

"How well the Holy Spirit spoke through the prophet
        Isaiah to your ancestors!
For he said,
    'Go and say to this people:
    You will listen and listen, but not understand;
    you will look and look, but not see,
    because this people's minds are dull,
    and they have stopped up their ears
    and closed their eyes.
    Otherwise, their eyes would see.
    their ears would hear,
    their minds would understand,
    and they would turn to me,
        says God,
    and I would heal them.' "

Acts 28:25b—27

Jesus Is Misunderstood by His Disciples in Galilee and Beyond _____ Mark 6:7—8:21

In the first part of the Gospel of Mark (1:1—3:6), Jesus was misunderstood by the scribes, the Pharisees, and the Herodians. In the second part (3:7—6:6), he was misunderstood by the people of his home area. In the third part (6:7—8:26), he is misunderstood even by his disciples. The disciples will really understand Jesus only when they accompany him on the way to Jerusalem and finally grasp the message of his death and resurrection in Jerusalem.

While the second part of the Gospel began with the choosing of the twelve disciples, the third part begins with Jesus sending them on a mission. The mission is an extension of Jesus' own activity. The disciples are to preach repentance, cast out demons, and heal the sick. Their power or authority to carry out this mission comes from Jesus, and the life-style they are asked to adopt is also that of Jesus.

Sandwiched between the sending out of the disciples and their return is the story of the death of John the Baptist. The activities of Jesus inspired many guesses about him. The King Herod in the story is Herod Antipas, the political ruler in Galilee from 4 B.C. (when Herod the Great, his father, died) to A.D. 39.

The guesses about who Jesus was, and Herod's belief that Jesus was John the Baptist restored to life, provide the occasion for telling the story of John's arrest and death. Herodias had been married to Herod Antipas' half brother named Herod also. Philip was married to Herodias' daughter Salome. These historical matters, however, should not distract from the more important points; John's death is a preview of the fate that awaits Jesus in Jerusalem.

These two accounts coming together suggest something further about the disciples' sharing in Jesus' life-style. The death of John the Baptist parallels Jesus' arrest and execution. To share in the mission of preaching the good news and joining battle with the power of evil is also to share in death and resurrection.

The possibility of imprisonment and death was all too real to the Christians of Mark's time. He indicates here that persecution is an expected outcome of discipleship. The return of the disciples sets the stage for the feeding of the 5,000.

■ Reflection

What items would be included in a list of things for modern disciples to bring with them on a missionary journey?

Jesus Sends Out the Twelve Disciples
(Also Matt. 10.5–15; Luke 9.1–6)

Then Jesus went to all the villages around there, teaching the people. ⁷He called the twelve disciples together and sent them out two by two. He gave them authority over the evil spirits ⁸and ordered them: "Don't take anything with you on the trip except a walking stick; no bread, no beggar's bag, no money in your pockets. ⁹Wear sandals, but don't wear an extra shirt." ¹⁰He also told them: "When you come to a town, stay with the people who receive you in their home until you leave that place. [11]If you come to a place where people do not welcome you or will not listen to you, leave it and shake the dust off your feet. This will be a warning to them!" [12]So they went out and preached that people should turn away from their sins. [13]They drove out many demons, and poured oil on many sick people and healed them.

The Death of John the Baptist
(Also Matt. 14.1–12; Luke 9.7–9)

[14]Now King Herod heard about all this, because Jesus' reputation had spread everywhere. Some people said, "John the Baptist has come back to life! That is why these powers are at work in him." [15]Others, however, said, "He is Elijah." Others said, "He is a prophet, like one of the prophets of long ago."

[16]When Herod heard it he said, "He is John the Baptist! I had his head cut off, but he has come back to life!" [17]Herod himself had ordered John's arrest, and had him tied up and put in prison. Herod did this because of Herodias, whom he had married, even though she was the wife of his brother Philip. [18]John the Baptist kept telling Herod: "It isn't right for you to marry your brother's wife!" [19]So Herodias held a grudge against John and wanted to kill him, but she couldn't because of Herod. [20]Herod was afraid of John because he knew that John was a good and holy man, and so he kept him safe. He liked to listen to him, even though he became greatly disturbed every time he heard him.

[21]Finally Herodias got her chance. It was on Herod's birthday, when he gave a feast for all

the top government officials, the military chiefs, and the leading citizens of Galilee. ²²The daughter of Herodias came in and danced, and pleased Herod and his guests. So the king said to the girl, "What would you like to have? I will give you anything you want." ²³With many vows he said to her, "I promise that I will give you anything you ask for, even as much as half my kingdom!" ²⁴So the girl went out and asked her mother, "What shall I ask for?" "The head of John the Baptist," she answered.

²⁵The girl hurried back at once to the king and demanded, "I want you to give me right now the head of John the Baptist on a plate!" ²⁶This made the king very sad; but he could not refuse her, because of the vows he had made in front of all his guests. ²⁷So he sent off a guard at once with orders to bring John's head. The guard left, went to the prison and cut John's head off; ²⁸then he brought it on a plate and gave it to the girl, who gave it to her mother. ²⁹When John's disciples heard about this, they came and got his body and laid it in a grave.

Jesus Feeds Five Thousand

The first part of the story (6:31-38) makes clear the many obstacles in the way to Jesus feeding such a large group of people. The point of enumerating the difficulties is that no natural means could be found to solve the problem of very little food for a very large crowd in an isolated place at a late hour. By the time the story concludes in 6:42-44, Mark points out that all these obstacles have been overcome through Jesus' miraculous power.

The story of the multiplication is rich in biblical symbolism, and this symbolism serves to relate the event to other important events narrated in Scripture. The multiplication takes place in a wilderness, as the manna was sent from God to feed the Israelites in the desert after the Exodus. In 2 Kings 4:42-44 Elisha feeds one hundred prophets with ten loaves and there is food left over. There are also many similarities in the language used in this narration and Mark's account of the Last Supper. A reading of Mark 14:22-25 as a companion to this section on the feeding of the 5,000 may give us added insight into the meaning of the Eucharist.

When Jews of Jesus' time talked about what things will be like when God's kingdom comes, they often used the image of the banquet. The Messiah presides at the banquet. Part of the menu is the sea creatures overcome by God in creation. 2 Baruch 29:3-4 (part of Jewish apocalyptic literature, this book narrates the visions ascribed to Baruch after the fall of Jerusalem to explain the tragedy and the suffering of the Jews) describes the banquet in this way: "Then the Messiah shall begin to be revealed. And Behemoth shall be revealed from his place and Leviathan shall ascend from the sea . . . and then they shall be food for all that are left." In other words, fish is food for the messianic banquet.

Understanding the various dimensions of the feeding of the 5,000—manna in the wilderness, Elisha's miracle, the anticipation of the Last Supper, the messianic banquet, the abundant feast for God's people—can add to the richness and depth of our celebrations of the Eucharist.

■ *Reflection*
Has our appreciation of the Eucharist been enhanced by our study of the Gospel? In what ways?

Jesus Feeds Five Thousand
(Also Matt. 14.13–21; Luke 9.10–17; John 6.1–14)

[30]The apostles returned and met with Jesus, and told him all they had done and taught. [31]There were so many people coming and going that Jesus and his disciples didn't even have time to eat. So he said to them, "Let us go off by ourselves to some place where we will be alone and you can rest a while." [32]So they started out in the boat by themselves to a lonely place.

[33]Many people, however, saw them leave and knew at once who they were; so they left from all the towns and ran ahead by land and got to the place ahead of Jesus and his disciples. [34]When Jesus got out of the boat, he saw this large crowd, and his heart was filled with pity for them, because they looked like sheep without a shepherd. So he began to teach them many things. [35]When it was getting late, his disciples came to him and said, "It is already very late, and this is a lonely place. [36]Send the people away, and let them go to the nearby farms and villages and buy themselves something to eat." [37]"You yourselves give them something to eat," Jesus answered. They asked, "Do you want us to go and buy two hundred dollars' worth of bread and feed them?" [38]So Jesus asked them, "How much bread do you have? Go and see." When they found out they told him, "Five loaves, and two fish also."

[39]Jesus then told his disciples to make all the people divide into groups and sit down on the green grass. [40]So the people sat down in rows, in groups of a hundred and groups of fifty. [41]Then Jesus took the five loaves and the two fish, looked up to heaven, and gave thanks

to God. He broke the loaves and gave them to his disciples to distribute to the people. He also divided the two fish among them all. ⁴²Everyone ate and had enough. ⁴³Then the disciples took up twelve baskets full of what was left of the bread and of the fish. ⁴⁴The number of men who ate the bread was five thousand.

Jesus Walks on Water

Jesus' display of power in feeding the 5,000 is followed by a story about his ability to walk on water and rescue his disciples from the dangers of the sea. There are three important features in this story: the superhuman identity of Jesus, his ability to rescue his followers, and the disciples' failure to understand him.

The expression "he was going to pass them by" in 6:48 is very important for understanding the meaning of the incident. Mark here suggests that Jesus is manifesting himself as Lord. In Exodus 33:17-23 Moses asks God to be with Israel and if he (Moses) can see God. God tells Moses that he can see him, but not completely. The Lord will "pass by," shielding Moses' vision of his face until he has passed. This section of Exodus would have been familiar to Jews of Mark's time in that it is part of the story of the giving of the law.

Other Old Testament passages like Isaiah 43:16, Job 9:8, Psalm 77:19 point out that it is the Lord God who has power over the waters, saving his people from the power of evil. A suggestion is being made about the divinity of Jesus.

In 6:51-52 the focus shifts from Jesus to the disciples. Mark relates the feeding of the 5,000 to their witnessing of Jesus walking on the water. The disciples are amazed—they have not yet grasped the true identity of Jesus.

The faith of the common people is highlighted in 6:53-56. The passage reminds us of the very positive reactions that met Jesus' miracles, and prepares for the conflict with the Pharisees and scribes in 7:1-23. The common people respond to Jesus in a positive way, but the religious experts are only interested in finding fault.

Jesus Walks on the Water
(Also Matt. 14.22–33; John 6.15–21)

[45]At once Jesus made his disciples get into the boat and go ahead of him to Bethsaida, on the other side of the lake, while he sent the crowd away. [46]After saying good-bye to the disciples, he went away to a hill to pray. [47]When evening came the boat was in the middle of the lake, while Jesus was alone on land. [48]He saw that his disciples were having trouble rowing the boat, because the wind was blowing against them; so sometime between three and six o'clock in the morning he came to them, walking on the water. He was going to pass them by. [49]But they saw him walking on the water. "It's a ghost!" they thought, and screamed. [50]For when they all saw him they were afraid.

Jesus spoke to them at once, "Courage!" he said. "It is I. Don't be afraid!" [51]Then he got into the boat with them, and the wind died down. The disciples were completely amazed and utterly confused. [52]They had not understood what these loaves of bread meant; their minds could not grasp it.

[53]They crossed the lake and came to land at Gennesaret, where they tied up the boat. [54]As they left the boat, people recognized Jesus at once. [55]So they ran throughout the whole region and brought the sick lying on their mats to

him, wherever they heard he was. ⁵⁶And everywhere Jesus went, to villages, towns, or farms, people would take their sick to the market places and beg him to let the sick at least touch the edge of his cloak; and all who touched it were made well.

Ritual Purity

As a Jewish religious teacher in Palestine, Jesus had to take a public position regarding the Pharisees and their teachings on ritual purity. Jesus' views are presented in 7:1-23. He is highly critical of the Pharisees. He not only accuses them of hypocrisy, but also appears to abolish all the regulations about clean and unclean foods.

The setting for the controversy is developed in 7:1-5. The Pharisees were a lay religious movement. They expressed their religious fellowship in communal meals, and hoped that all Jews would observe the Old Testament rules of priestly ritual purity. The scribes were experts in the interpretation of the Old Testament laws and their application to everyday life. The Pharisees and scribes were not necessarily distinct groups, since some of the Pharisees may also have been scribes. In modern Catholic terms, the Pharisees were members of a religious group (like Jesuits) and the scribes were religious intellectuals (like theologians). The point at issue in the controversy is ritual purity, not hygiene. The opponents wonder why the disciples of Jesus were not sharing in the pharisaic program of ritual holiness.

In 7:3-4 Mark describes the Pharisees' program. He explains it in terms of tradition. Since the first audience for the Gospel was a mixture of Jewish and gentile converts to Christianity, Mark finds it necessary to explain more fully the customs of ritual washing. The discussion comes even more into focus when we realize that a major point of controversy in the early Church was over whether gentiles should be made to observe the Jewish laws and traditions in order to become Christians.

In 7:5 the basic point of the controversy is stated in the form of a question. Jesus' direct response to the Pharisees and scribes appears in 7:6-13. He calls the opponents "hypocrites." That word originally described actors who wore masks while playing their roles on stage. Here it means something like our word "phonies." In this harsh judgment, Jesus quotes from Isaiah 29:13.

The thrust of Jesus' criticism is made clear in 7:8. The opponents are so insistent on observing their traditions that they disregard the commandments of God. In 7:9-13 Jesus gives an example of an actual conflict between divine command and a tradition accepted by the opponents. The divine command is the so-called fourth commandment: Honor your father and your mother (Exodus 20:12; Deuteronomy 5:16). The negative version is also quoted: He who speaks evil of father or mother, let him surely die (Exodus 21:17; Leviticus 20:9). The tradition is the practice of "corban," which allowed a person to declare a property as an offering to God and thus evade the obligation of contributing to the support of one's aged parents.

The second and most radical part of Jesus' teaching appears in 7:14-23. Jesus is understood to be overturning centuries of tradition regarding dietary laws which the Jews believed in as passed down from Moses. For Christians there would be a clear break with those traditions. But there is also in Mark an emphasis placed on the contrast between ritual cleanliness and cleanliness of the heart. What one eats or how one eats is of little consequence compared to how one speaks and acts.

The Teaching of the Ancestors
(Also Matt. 15.1–9)

7 The Pharisees and some teachers of the Law who had come from Jerusalem gathered around Jesus. ²They noticed that some of his disciples were eating their food with "unclean" hands—that is, they had not washed them in the way the Pharisees said people should.

(³For the Pharisees, as well as the rest of the Jews, follow the teaching they received from their ancestors: they don't eat unless they wash their hands in the proper way, ⁴nor do they eat anything that comes from the market unless they wash it first. And they follow many other rules which they have received, such as the proper way to wash cups, pots, copper bowls, and beds.)

⁵So the Pharisees and the teachers of the Law asked Jesus, "Why is it that your disciples do not follow the teaching handed down by our ancestors, but instead eat with unclean hands?" ⁶Jesus answered them: "How right Isaiah was when he prophesied about you! You are hypocrites, just as he wrote:
> 'These people, says God, honor me with their words,
> But their heart is really far away from me.
⁷It is no use for them to worship me,
> Because they teach man-made commandments as though they were God's rules!' "
⁸And Jesus said, "You put aside the commandment of God and obey the teachings of men."

⁹And Jesus continued: "You have a clever way of rejecting God's law in order to uphold your own teaching!

¹⁰For Moses commanded, 'Honor your father and mother,' and, 'Anyone who says bad things about his father or mother must be put to death.' ¹¹But you teach that if a person has something he could use to help his father or mother, but says, 'This is Corban' (which means, it belongs to God), ¹²he is excused from helping his father or mother. ¹³In this way you disregard the word of God with the teaching you pass on to others. And there are many other things of this kind that you do.''

¹⁴Then Jesus called the crowd to him once more and said to them: ''Listen to me, all of you, and understand. ¹⁵There is nothing that goes into a person from the outside which can make him unclean. Rather, it is what comes out of a person that makes him unclean. [¹⁶Listen, then, if you have ears to hear with!]''

¹⁷When he left the crowd and went into the house, his disciples asked him about this parable. ¹⁸''You are no more intelligent than the others,'' Jesus said to them. ''Don't you understand? Nothing that goes into a person from the outside can really make him unclean, ¹⁹because it does not go into his heart but into his stomach and then goes on out of the body.'' (In saying this Jesus declared that all foods are fit to be eaten.) ²⁰And he went on to say: ''It is what comes out of a person that makes him unclean. ²¹For from the inside, from a man's heart, come the evil ideas which lead him to do immoral things, to rob, kill, ²²commit adultery, covet, and do all sorts of evil things; deceit, indecency, jealousy, slander, pride, and folly—²³all these evil things come from inside a man and make him unclean.''

Healings

The lack of understanding shown by Jesus' opponents and even by his disciples is contrasted in 7:24-30 by the understanding and faith shown by a non-Jewish woman in an area outside of Palestine. Again Mark is addressing a controversy among Jewish and gentile Christians of his time.

Another healing story is presented in 7:31-37. Many of the same elements that were manifest in earlier healing stories are present here. By means of a reference to an Old Testament passage (here it is Isaiah 35:5-6), Jesus is revealed to the reader to be the Messiah. He instructs the witnesses to keep silent about the miracle, but they cannot. He is perceived to be the Son of God.

A Woman's Faith
(Also Matt. 15.21–28)

²⁴Then Jesus left and went away to the territory near the city of Tyre. He went into a house, and did not want anyone to know he was there; but he could not stay hidden. ²⁵A certain woman, whose daughter had an evil spirit in her, heard about Jesus and came to him at once and fell at his feet. ²⁶The woman was a foreigner, born in Phoenicia of Syria. She begged Jesus to drive the demon out of her daughter. ²⁷But Jesus answered, "Let us feed the children first; it isn't right to take the children's food and throw it to the dogs." ²⁸"Sir," she answered, "even the dogs under the table eat the children's leftovers!" ²⁹So Jesus said to her, "For such an answer you may go home; the demon has gone out of your daughter!" ³⁰So she went back home and there found her child lying on the bed; the demon had indeed gone out of her.

³¹Jesus then left the neighborhood of Tyre and went on through Sidon to Lake Galilee, going by way of the territory of the Ten Towns. ³²Some people brought him a man who was deaf and could hardly speak, and begged Jesus to place his hand on him. ³³So Jesus took him off alone, away from the crowd, put his fingers in the man's ears, spat, and touched the man's tongue. ³⁴Then Jesus looked up to heaven, gave a deep groan, and said to the man, *Ephphatha,* which means, "Open up!" ³⁵At once the man's ears were opened, his tongue was set loose, and he began to talk without any trouble. ³⁶Then Jesus ordered them all not to speak of it to anyone; but the more he ordered them, the more they told it. ³⁷And all who heard were completely amazed. "How well he does everything!" they exclaimed. "He even makes the deaf to hear and the dumb to speak!"

Jesus Feeds Four Thousand

The conditions here are much the same as with the feeding of the 5,000 in chapter 6. The parallels with the Last Supper are also apparent. Even the number of baskets of leftovers is symbolic. In the first instance there were twelve baskets left over, in this case there are seven. In ancient numerology these numbers were associated with perfection and divinity. There may be some connection with the twelve tribes of Israel, and the seven(ty) nations of the world outside Israel.

In both instances of multiplication of bread, there is also the element of Jesus' compassion on those who follow him faithfully. Mark intends to communicate to his contemporaries that Jesus will not leave his disciples hungry in the wilderness of persecution. Like the Israelites in the desert, they will be nourished through the power of the Lord.

Jesus Feeds Four Thousand
(Also Matt. 15.32–39)

8 Not long afterward, another large crowd came together. When they had nothing left to eat, Jesus called the disciples to him and said: ²"I feel sorry for these people, because they have been with me for three days and now have nothing to eat. ³If I send them home without feeding them they will faint as they go, because some of them have come a long way." ⁴His disciples asked him, "Where in this desert can anyone find enough food to feed all these people?" ⁵"How much bread do you have?" Jesus asked. "Seven loaves," they answered.

⁶He ordered the crowd to sit down on the ground. Then he took the seven loaves, gave thanks to God, broke them, and gave them to his disciples to distribute to the crowd; and the disciples did so. ⁷They also had a few small fish. Jesus gave thanks for these and told the disciples to distribute them too. ⁸Everybody ate and had enough—there were about four thousand people. ⁹Then the disciples took up seven baskets full of pieces left over. Jesus sent the people away, ¹⁰and at once got into the boat with his disciples and went to the district of Dalmanutha.

Jesus Responds to Unbelief

This third section concludes with Jesus even more at odds with his opponents, and with little support from his chosen disciples. Mark continues to stress the contrast between those to whom special responsibility for faith has been given, and the common people, Jew and gentile, who witnessed and better understood what was happening in their midst.

■ Reflection

In what ways can we help our faith in Jesus to grow?

The Pharisees Ask for a Miracle
(Also Matt. 16.1–4)

¹¹Some Pharisees came up and started to argue with Jesus. They wanted to trap him, so they asked him to perform a miracle to show God's approval. ¹²Jesus gave a deep groan and said: "Why do the people of this day ask for a miracle? No, I tell you! No such proof will be given this people!" ¹³He left them, got back into the boat, and started across to the other side of the lake.

¹⁴The disciples had forgotten to bring any extra bread, and had only one loaf with them in the boat. ¹⁵"Look out," Jesus warned them, "and be on your guard against the yeast of the Pharisees and the yeast of Herod." ¹⁶They started discussing among themselves: "He says this because we don't have any bread." ¹⁷Jesus knew what they were saying, so he asked them: "Why are you discussing about not having any bread? Don't you know or understand yet? Are your minds so dull? ¹⁸You have eyes—can't you see? You have ears—can't you hear? Don't you remember ¹⁹when I broke the five loaves for the five thousand people? How many baskets full of leftover pieces did you take up?" "Twelve," they answered. ²⁰"And when I broke the seven loaves for the four thousand people," asked Jesus, "how many baskets full of leftover pieces did you take up?" "Seven," they answered. ²¹"And you still don't understand?" he asked them.

■ Discussion

1. How is the Christian concept of discipleship developed in this section of Mark's Gospel?
2. How does the fate of John the Baptist anticipate the fate of Jesus?
3. How do the stories of the multiplication of loaves and fishes form a bridge from the Old Testament appreciation of the Exodus to the New Testament teaching on the Eucharist?
4. Is there a difference between the reaction to Jesus the wonder-worker and Jesus the teacher?
5. Does anyone show real faith in Jesus?

■ Prayer and Meditation

"The LORD is my Shepherd;
     I have everthing I need.
He lets me rest in fields of green grass
     and leads me to quiet pools of fresh water.
He gives me new strength.
He guides me in the right paths,
     as he has promised.
Even if I go through the deepest darkness.
     I will not be afraid, LORD
     for you are with me.
Your shepherd's rod and staff protect me.

You prepare a banquet for me,
     where all my enemies can see me;
you welcome me as an honored guest
     and fill my cup to the brim.
I know that your goodness and love will be with me all
          my life;
     and your house will be my home
          as long as I live."

Psalm 23:1–6

Jesus' Instructions to His Disciples on the Way to Jerusalem———— Mark 8:22—10:52

The disciples' misunderstandings about Jesus are corrected as they journey from Caesarea Philippi in northern Galilee to Jerusalem, the place in which Jesus will die. The major themes of the instruction given by Jesus along the way are Christology (who Jesus is) and discipleship (who the followers of Jesus are). The journey begins and ends with stories about Jesus' ability to give sight to the blind (8:22-26; 10:46-52). The journey is presented according to a pattern that is repeated three times: a geographical reference (8:27; 9:30; 10:32), a prediction of Jesus' death and resurrection (8:31; 9:31; 10:33-34), a misunderstanding on the part of the disciples (8:32-33; 9:32-34; 10:35-41), and teachings that correct the disciples' misunderstandings (8:34—9:1; 9:35-37; 10:42-45). Other teachings on various topics are included in the intervening passages.

The Blind Man at Bethsaida

The story of the healing of the blind man at Bethsaida is not intended simply as a display of Jesus' power as a wonder-worker. Rather it gains spiritual depth by its closeness to Jesus' challenge to the disciples in 8:18: "You have eyes—can't you see?"

Perhaps the two-stage process of the restoration of the man's sight implies something about the gradual nature of disciples' coming to a clearer understanding about Jesus.

Jesus Heals a Blind Man at Bethsaida

[22]They came to Bethsaida, where some people brought a blind man to Jesus and begged him to touch him. [23]Jesus took the blind man by the hand and led him out of the village. After spitting on the man's eyes, Jesus placed his hands on him and asked him, "Can you see anything?" [24]The man looked up and said, "I can see men, but they look like trees walking around." [25]Jesus again placed his hands on the man's eyes. This time the man looked hard, his eyesight came back, and he saw everything clearly. [26]Jesus then sent him home with the order, "Don't go back into the village."

The Passion Predicted

The first instance of the four-part pattern appears in 8:27-9:1: the geographical reference, the passion prediction, the misunderstanding by the disciples, and the correction by Jesus. Caesarea Philippi was about twenty-five miles north of the Sea of Galilee. The journey begins at the northern tip of the land of Israel and heads toward Jerusalem. The first topic for discussion on the way is the identity of Jesus in 8:27-30.

The Greek word *Christos* means "anointed," and its Hebrew equivalent is Messiah. In the early parts of the Old Testament the term "anointed" was applied to kings and priests. At the time of Jesus it described an agent of God who would come from the house of David and deliver Israel from its enemies and establish a world empire marked by peace and justice. But Jesus was not that kind of Messiah.

The first passion prediction appears in 8:31. Here Peter, who had unhesitatingly identified Jesus as the Messiah, is unable to comprehend the need for his death and resurrection. When Jesus places Peter on the side of Satan, he is expressing something about his own position in the cosmic struggle between good and evil.

Peter's misconception of Jesus is corrected in the instruction in 8:34—9:1. Here there is a double level of meaning to Jesus' instruction. The first audience is the disciples and the crowd. The second is the Christian community in Mark's time, persecuted and suffering for their faith. Mark emphasizes that suffering is part of discipleship.

■ *Reflection*
What practical guidelines for life within the Church today can be found in Jesus' instructions to the disciples?

Peter's Declaration About Jesus
(Also Matt. 16.13–20; Luke 9.18–21)

[27]Then Jesus and his disciples went away to the villages of Caesarea Philippi. On the way he asked them, "Tell me, who do people say I am?" [28]"Some say that you are John the Baptist," they answered; "others say that you are Elijah, while others say that you are one of the prophets."

[29]"What about you?" he asked them. "Who do you say I am?" Peter answered, "You are the Messiah" [30]Then Jesus ordered them, "Do not tell anyone about me."

³¹Then Jesus began to teach his disciples: "The Son of Man must suffer much, and be rejected by the elders, the chief priests, and the teachers of the Law. He will be put to death, and after three days he will be raised to life." ³²He made this very clear to them. So Peter took him aside and began to rebuke him. ³³But Jesus turned around, looked at his disciples, and rebuked Peter. "Get away from me, Satan," he said. "Your thoughts are men's thoughts, not God's!"

³⁴Then Jesus called the crowd and his disciples to him. "If anyone wants to come with me," he told them, "he must forget himself, carry his cross, and follow me. ³⁵For the man who wants to save his own life will lose it; but the man who loses his life for me and for the gospel will save it. ³⁶Does a man gain anything if he wins the whole world but loses his life? Of course not! ³⁷There is nothing a man can give to regain his life. ³⁸If, then, a man is ashamed of me and of my teaching in this godless and wicked day, then the Son of Man will be ashamed of him when he comes in the glory of his Father with the holy angels."

9 And he went on to say: "Remember this! There are some here who will not die until they have seen the Kingdom of God come with power."

The Transfiguration and a Healing

Whatever the original meaning of the saying in 9:1 may have been, the transfiguration of Jesus is presented as an anticipation or preview of the kingdom of God come with power. The reference to "after six days" may simply be part of the traditional story, although it may also have some connection with the appearance of God's glory to Moses on Sinai in Exodus 24:15-18. The two events are certainly similar in that they both take place on high mountains, and there is a divine manifestation. During the transfiguration account the heavenly voice proclaims Jesus as the Son of God as it did at his baptism.

The descent from the mountain shows that the disciples still do not understand Jesus. It also answers the objection that Jesus could not be the Messiah because Elijah had not yet come. Based on Malachi 3:1 and 4:5, the common belief was that Elijah had to come before the Messiah. Here Jesus equates John the Baptist with Elijah, a reference Mark makes in chapter 1.

As Jews of this period in history, the disciples would certainly know what rising from the dead meant (9:9). But they could not have been expected to understand why the Messiah had to die in order to be raised from the dead, or how one person rather than all humanity could be raised before the end of time.

In the story of the healing of the boy with the unclean spirit (9:14-29), the first part focuses on the disciples and their inability to cure the boy. In the second part, attention shifts to Jesus and the boy's father. In the third part attention turns again to the disciples. The sandwhich technique used here is effective in bringing out the contrast between the faith of the boy's father and the unbelief of the other witnesses.

The Transfiguration
(Also Matt. 17.1–13; Luke 9.28–36)

²Six days later Jesus took Peter, James, and John with him, and led them up a high mountain by themselves. As they looked on, a change came over him, ³and his clothes became very shining and white; nobody in the world

could clean them as white. ⁴Then the three disciples saw Elijah and Moses, who were talking with Jesus. ⁵Peter spoke up and said to Jesus: "Teacher, it is a good thing that we are here. We will make three tents, one for you, one for Moses, and one for Elijah." ⁶He and the others were so frightened that he did not know what to say. ⁷A cloud appeared and covered them with its shadow, and a voice came from the cloud: "This is my own dear Son—listen to him!" ⁸They took a quick look around but did not see anybody else; only Jesus was with them.

⁹As they came down the mountain Jesus ordered them: "Don't tell anyone what you have seen, until the Son of Man has been raised from death." ¹⁰They obeyed his order, but among themselves they started discussing the matter: "What does this 'rising from death' mean? ¹¹And they asked Jesus: "Why do the teachers of the Law say that Elijah has to come first?" ¹²His answer was: "Elijah does indeed come first to get everything ready. Yet why do the Scriptures say that the Son of Man will suffer much and be rejected? ¹³I tell you, however, that Elijah has already come, and that people did to him all they wanted to, just as the Scriptures say about him."

Jesus Heals a Boy with an Evil Spirit
(Also Matt. 17.14–21; Luke 9.37–43a)

¹⁴When they joined the rest of the disciples, they saw a large crowd there. Some teachers of the Law were arguing with the disciples. ¹⁵As soon as the people saw Jesus, they were greatly surprised and ran to him and greeted him. ¹⁶Jesus asked his disciples. "What are you

arguing with them about?" [17]A man in the crowd answered: "Teacher, I brought my son to you, because he has an evil spirit in him and cannot talk. [18]Whenever the spirit attacks him, it throws him to the ground and he foams at the mouth, grits his teeth, and becomes stiff all over. I asked your disciples to drive the spirit out, but they could not." [19]Jesus said to them: "How unbelieving you people are! How long must I stay with you? How long do I have to put up with you? Bring the boy to me." [20]And they brought him to Jesus. As soon as the spirit saw Jesus, it threw the boy into a fit, so that he fell on the ground and rolled around, foaming at the mouth. [21]"How long has he been like this?" Jesus asked the father. "Ever since he was a child," he replied. [22]"Many times it has tried to kill him by throwing him in the fire and in the water. Have pity on us and help us, if you possibly can!" [23]"Yes," said Jesus, "if *you* can! Everything is possible for the person who has faith." [24]The father at once cried out, "I do have faith, but not enough. Help me!"

[25]Jesus noticed that the crowd was closing in on them, so he gave a command to the evil spirit. "Deaf and dumb spirit," he said, "I order you to come out of the boy and never go into him again!" [26]With a scream the spirit threw the boy into a bad fit and came out. The boy looked like a corpse, so that everybody said, "He is dead!" [27]But Jesus took the boy by the hand and helped him rise, and he stood up.

[28]After Jesus had gone indoors, his disciples asked him privately: "Why couldn't we drive the spirit out?" [29]"Only prayer can drive this kind out," answered Jesus; "nothing else can."

The Second Passion Prediction

The second instance of the four-part pattern appears in 9:30-37: the geographical reference (9:30), the passion prediction (9:31), the misunderstanding by the disciples (9:32-34), and the correction by Jesus (9:35-37). Jesus and the disciples are now heading south through Galilee toward Jerusalem. Jesus intends to give exclusive time to the disciples, who still have great difficulty in understanding his predictions of the passion and the resurrection.

The disciples' lack of understanding is developed by their conversation on the way. There is evidence in the Dead Sea scrolls and other Jewish writings of the time of a keen interest in status or rank in the coming kingdom of God. Since Jesus preached mainly about the coming of God's kingdom, the disciples' conversation probably concerned their places in that kingdom. They still fail to understand the service of Jesus.

Jesus compares the true disciple to a child. In Jewish society of Jesus' time, children had no legal rights, were totally dependent on parents or guardians, and thus had no social status or rank. The child here symbolizes the fact that no one has a right or a claim on God's kingdom. It is a gift, and it is God's privilege to give it. The child is not presented here as a symbol of innocence or humility or natural goodness.

Jesus Speaks Again About His Death
(Also Matt. 17.22–23; Luke 9.43b–45)

³⁰They left that place and went on through Galilee. Jesus did not want anyone to know where he was, ³¹because he was teaching his disciples: "The Son of Man will be handed over to men who will kill him; three days later, how-

ever, he will be raised to life." ³²They did not understand what this teaching meant, but they were afraid to ask him.

³³They came to Capernaum, and after going indoors Jesus asked his disciples: "What were you arguing about on the road?" ³⁴But they would not answer him, because on the road they had been arguing among themselves about who was the greatest. ³⁵Jesus sat down, called the twelve disciples and said to them: "Whoever wants to be first must place himself last of all and be the servant of all." ³⁶He took a child and made him stand in front of them. Then he put his arms around him and said to them, ³⁷"The person who in my name welcomes one of these children, welcomes me; and whoever welcomes me, welcomes not only me but also the one who sent me."

Further Instructions

The report of an exorcist acting in Jesus' name in 9:38-41 provides the occasion for further instructions about the community formed by Jesus. The saying in 9:41 is related to 9:38-40 on the purely formal basis of the word "name." The strange exorcist casts out demons in the name of Jesus (see Acts 8:18; 19:13), and someone gives a cup of water in the name of Christ.

Another verbal connection is developed between the saying about the child in 9:37 and the warning against scandalizing or causing little ones to sin in 9:42, and this idea of scandal is then taken up in 9:43-48. The final saying in 9:47-48 contains the word "fire," and this word attracts the saying in 9:49, which in turn attracts the saying about salt in 9:50. This purely formal technique of composition probably reflects the oral phase of the Gospel tradition.

The expression "purified by fire" in 9:49 may refer to the persecution and suffering that face the community. The word "salt" in 9:50 is apparently used in the sense of spiritual understanding.

■ *Reflection*

Is there evidence that Jesus is still misunderstood by his present-day disciples?

Who Is Not Against Us Is For Us
(Also Luke 9.49–50)

³⁸John said to him, "Teacher, we saw a man who was driving out demons in your name, and we told him to stop, because he doesn't belong to our group." ³⁹"Do not try to stop him," answered Jesus, "because no one who performs a miracle in my name will be able soon after to say bad things about me. ⁴⁰For whoever is not against us is for us. ⁴¹Remember this! Anyone who gives you a drink of water because you belong to Christ will certainly receive his reward."

⁴²"As for these little ones who believe in me—it would be better for a man to have a large millstone tied around his neck and be thrown into the sea, than for him to cause one of them to turn away from me. ⁴³So if your hand makes you turn away, cut it off! It is better for you to enter life without a hand than to keep both hands and go off to hell, to the fire that never goes out. [⁴⁴There 'their worms never die, and the fire is never put out.'] ⁴⁵And if your foot makes you turn away, cut it off! It is better for you to enter life without a foot than to keep both feet and be thrown into hell. [⁴⁶There 'their worms never die, and the fire is never put out.'] ⁴⁷And if your eye makes you turn away, take it out! It is better for you to enter the Kingdom of

out! It is better for you to enter the Kingdom of God with only one eye, than to keep both eyes and be thrown into hell. [⁴⁸There 'their worms never die, and the fire is never put out.']

⁴⁹"For everyone will be salted with fire. ⁵⁰Salt is good. But if it loses its saltiness, how can you make it salty again? Have salt in yourselves, and be at peace with one another."

Marriage and Divorce

Jesus' comment on marriage and divorce is presented in 10:1-12. It takes place as the journey undertaken by Jesus and his disciples leaves Galilee and enters Judea and the area across the Jordan River. Jerusalem, which is the goal of the journey and the place of Jesus' death, is in the region of Judea.

The topic of divorce is raised by the Pharisees in 10:2. Jesus tells them to repeat what Moses commanded them. Their reply is based on Deuteronomy 24:1. There was some debate among Jewish scholars of Jesus' time over the Old Testament phrase "some indecency." One school interpreted it freely as any lack or failure on the woman's part that displeased the husband, while another school confined it to adultery on the woman's part. Jesus takes neither position and calls into question the very basis of the debate.

Jesus' teaching on marriage and divorce is given in 10:5-9. The "man" mentioned in 10:9 is most likely the husband, since in Jewish law the husband instituted the divorce proceeding against the wife and no third party was needed.

In case Jesus' teaching in 10:5-9 had not been clearly understood, it is presented again for the disciples in 10:11-12. The precise nature of the exception introduced in Matthew 5:32 and 19:9 is a matter of long debate. It may refer to sexual misconduct or marriage within the forbidden degrees of kinship (with a first cousin or a sister).

There is little doubt that Jesus regarded marriage as indissoluble, and that his teaching was as radical and controversial then as it is now. It is also significant that in the Matthean and Pauline texts Jesus' teaching is modified to some extent (see Corinthians 7:10-11).

Jesus Teaches About Divorce
(Also Matt. 19.1–12; Luke 16.18)

10 Then Jesus left that place, went to the region of Judea, and crossed the Jordan river. Again crowds came flocking to him and he taught them, as he always did.

²Some Pharisees came to him and tried to trap him. "Tell us," they asked, "does our Law allow a man to divorce his wife?" ³Jesus answered with a question: "What commandment did Moses give you?" ⁴Their answer was, "Moses gave permission for a man to write a divorce notice and send his wife away." ⁵Jesus said to them: "Moses wrote this commandment for you because you are so hard to teach. ⁶But in the beginning, at the time of creation, it was said, 'God made them male and female. ⁷And for this reason a man will leave his father and mother and unite with his wife, ⁸and the two will become one. So they are no longer two, but one. ⁹Man must not separate, then, what God has joined together."

¹⁰When they went back into the house, the disciples asked Jesus about this matter. ¹¹He said to them: "The man who divorces his wife and marries another woman commits adultery against his wife; ¹²in the same way, the woman who divorces her husband and marries another man commits adultery."

The Meaning of Discipleship

The story of the blessing of the children in 10:13-16 really concerns the kingdom of God and the attitude that should be taken toward it. It must be received as a gift. The conversation with the rich man in 10:17-22 illustrates what being a disciple of Jesus may demand. Jesus goes on to present the positive side of following him in poverty. Again, these words are meant as support for Mark's community of Christians facing hardship for their belief in Christ.

Jesus Blesses Little Children
(Also Matt. 19.13–15; Luke 18.15–17)

¹³Some people brought children to Jesus for him to touch them, but the disciples scolded those people. ¹⁴When Jesus noticed it, he was angry and said to his disciples: "Let the children come to me! Do not stop them, because the Kingdom of God belongs to such as these. ¹⁵Remember this! Whoever does not receive the Kingdom of God like a child will never enter it." ¹⁶Then he took the children in his arms, placed his hands on each of them, and blessed them.

¹⁷As Jesus was starting again on his way, a man ran up, knelt before him, and asked him: "Good Teacher, what must I do to receive eternal life?" ¹⁸"Why do you call me good?" Jesus

asked him. "No one is good except God alone. [19]You know the commandments: 'Do not murder; do not commit adultery; do not steal; do not lie; do not cheat; honor your father and mother.' "

[20]"Teacher," the man said, "ever since I was young I have obeyed all these commandments." [21]With love Jesus looked straight at him and said: "You need only one thing. Go and sell all you have and give the money to the poor, and you will have riches in heaven; then come and follow me." [22]When the man heard this, gloom spread over his face and he went away sad, because he was very rich.

[23]Jesus looked around at his disciples and said to them, "How hard it will be for the rich people to enter the Kingdom of God!" [24]The disciples were shocked at these words, but Jesus went on to say: "My children, how hard it is to enter the Kingdom of God! [25]It is much harder for a rich man to enter the Kingdom of God than for a camel to go through the eye of a needle." [26]At this the disciples were completely amazed, and asked one another. "Who, then, can be saved?" [27]Jesus looked straight at them and answered: "This is impossible for men, but not for God; everything is possible for God."

[28]Then Peter spoke up: "Look, we have left everything and followed you." [29]"Yes," Jesus said to them, "and I tell you this: anyone who leaves home or brothers or sisters or mother or father or children or fields for me, and for the gospel, [30]will receive much more in this present age. He will receive a hundred times more houses, brothers, sisters, mothers, children, and fields—and persecutions as well; and in the age to come he will receive eternal life. [31]But many who now are first will be last, and many who now are last will be first."

The Third Passion Prediction

The third instance of the four-part pattern appears in 10:32-45: the geographical reference (10:32), the passion prediction (10:33-34), the misunderstanding by the disciples (10:35-37), and the correction by Jesus (10:38-45). The misunderstanding by the disciples again involves the issue of status or rank in the kingdom of God. Here James and John show little more understanding than the rest of the disciples, even though they have been present with Jesus during events which should have heightened their consciousness of what he was preaching.

Jesus' correction proceeds in three parts. In the first part (10:38-39), Jesus refers to his future sufferings and death by means of the images of the cup and the baptism. He will drink the cup of suffering and undergo the "drowning" of death. In the second part (10:40) Jesus denies that he can assign places of privilege in the kingdom. In the third part (10:41-45), Jesus explains what real leadership in his community means: it means service.

Jesus Speaks a Third Time About His Death
(Also Matt. 20.17—19; Luke 18.31—34)

[32]They were now on the road going up to Jerusalem. Jesus was going ahead of the disciples, who were filled with alarm; the people who followed behind were afraid. Once again Jesus took the twelve disciples aside and spoke of the things that were going to happen to him. [33]"Look," Jesus told them, "we are going up to Jerusalem where the Son of Man will be handed over to the chief priests and the teachers of the Law. They will condemn him to death and then hand him over to the Gentiles. [34]These

will make fun of him, spit on him, whip him, and kill him. And after three days he will be raised to life."

The Request of James and John
(Also Matt. 20.20—28)

³⁵Then James and John, the sons of Zebedee, came to Jesus. "Teacher," they said, "there is something we want you to do for us." ³⁶"What do you want me to do for you?" Jesus asked them. ³⁷They answered: "When you sit on your throne in the glorious Kingdom, we want you to let us sit with you, one at your right, and one at your left." ³⁸Jesus said to them: "You don't know what you are asking for. Can you drink the cup that I must drink? Can you be baptized in the way I must be baptized? ³⁹"We can," they answered. Jesus said to them: "You will indeed drink the cup I must drink and be baptized in the way I must be baptized. ⁴⁰But I do not have the right to choose who will sit at my right and my left. It is God who will give these places to those for whom he has prepared them."

⁴¹When the other ten disciples heard about this they became angry with James and John. ⁴²So Jesus called them all together to him and said: "You know that the men who are considered rulers of the people have power over them, and the leaders rule over them. ⁴³This, however, is not the way it is among you. If one of you wants to be great, he must be the servant of the rest; ⁴⁴and if one of you wants to be first, he must be the slave of all. ⁴⁵For even the Son of Man did not come to be served; he came to serve and to give his life to redeem many people."

The Blind Bartimaeus

This part of the Gospel ends just as it began—with Jesus giving sight to a blind man. In their present context, both stories have to do with spiritual insight and understanding as well as physical healing. This healing takes place near Jericho, not very far from Jerusalem. The blind beggar Bartimaeus calls Jesus "Son of David." Bartimaeus becomes a symbol for the true disciples of Jesus. He understands Jesus' identity. His faith in Jesus leads to a cure for his blindness. Once he can see, he follows Jesus.

■ *Reflection*

Does the journey from Galilee to Jerusalem have any parallel in the spiritual journey of most Christians?

Jesus Heals Blind Bartimaeus
(Also Matt. 20.29–34; Luke 18.35–43)

[46]They came to Jericho. As Jesus was leaving with his disciples and a large crowd, a blind man named Bartimaeus, the son of Timaeus, was sitting and begging by the road. [47]When he heard that it was Jesus of Nazareth, he began to shout, "Jesus! Son of David! Have mercy on me!" [48]Many scolded him and told him to be quiet. But he shouted even more loudly, "Son of David, have mercy on me!" [49]Jesus stopped and said, "Call him." So they called the blind man. "Cheer up!" they said. "Get up, he is calling you." [50]He threw off his cloak, jumped up and came to Jesus. [51]"What do you want me to do for you?" Jesus asked him. "Teacher," the blind man answered, "I want to see again." [52]"Go," Jesus told him, "your faith has made you well." At once he was able to see, and followed Jesus on the road.

■ Discussion

1. How does the miraculous bestowal of sight in 8:22-26 prepare for the journey from northern Galilee to Jerusalem?

2. How does Jesus present himself and his destiny?

3. Are the disciples going forward or backward in their understanding of Jesus?

4. Based on Mark's Gospel to this point, how would you describe the kingdom of God?

5. How does the miraculous bestowal of sight in 10:46-52 summarize the journey from Galilee to Jerusalem? How does it prepare for the events that will take place in Jerusalem?

■ Prayer and Meditation

"Everyone will see the LORD'S splendor,
    see his greatness and power.

The blind will be able to see,
    and the deaf will hear.

The lame will leap and dance,
    and those who cannot speak will shout for joy.

Streams of water will flow through the desert;
    the burning sand will become a lake,
    and dry land will be filled with springs."

Isaiah 35:2b,5–7

Jesus' Deeds and Words in Jerusalem —Mark 11:1—13:37

The material in chapters 11-13 is presented according to an outline of three days (11:1-11; 11:12-19; 11:20 —13:37), and special emphasis is placed on Jesus' teaching activity in the area of the Jerusalem Temple. One day prepares for the next. The first day focuses on the identity of Jesus, and the second day treats the demand that God's people repent. The third day clarifies and unites those themes: Jesus the Son of God demands conversion to the correct understanding of God and to right relationship with other people.

The First Day

The story of the entrance into Jerusalem (11:1-11) emphasizes and develops Jesus' identity as the son of David, which was confessed publicly by Bartimaeus in 10:46-52. From the area just outside of Jerusalem, Jesus sends two disciples to get a colt on which he will ride into Jerusalem. A reading of Zechariah 9:9 and 14:4 will shed some light on the meaning of Jesus' entry from the Mount of Olives on a colt.

Mark does not describe a huge crowd. Mark may have understood the entrance as a demonstration undertaken by Jesus and the disciples.

Recall the broad geographical outline of the Gospel. Jesus began his public activity in Galilee, proclaiming the kingdom and the need for repentance. As he enters Jerusalem, his followers proclaim the coming of the kingdom. All along his progress from Galilee to Jerusalem, Jesus is received enthusiastically by the common people, but challenged by religious leaders and misunderstood by his own disciples. This will also be true in Jerusalem.

■ *Reflection*

Why do you think the Church includes both the stories of the entry into Jerusalem and the passion in the Palm Sunday liturgy?

The Triumphant Entry into Jerusalem
(Also Matt. 21.1–11; Luke 19.28–40; John 12.12–19)

11 As they came near Jerusalem, at the towns of Bethphage and Bethany they came to the Mount of Olives. Jesus sent two of his disciples on ahead ²with these instructions: "Go to the village there ahead of you. As soon as you get there you will find a colt tied up that has never been ridden. Untie it and bring it here. ³And if someone asks you, 'Why are you doing that?' tell him. 'The Master needs it and will send it back here at once.' " ⁴So they went and found a colt out in the street, tied to the door of a house. As they were untying it, ⁵some of the bystanders asked them, "What are you doing, untying that colt?" ⁶They answered just as Jesus had told them, so the men let them go. ⁷They brought the colt to Jesus, threw their cloaks over the animal, and Jesus got on. ⁸Many people spread their cloaks on the road, while others cut branches in the fields and spread them on the road. ⁹The people who were in front and those who followed behind began to shout, "Praise God! God bless him who comes in the name of the Lord! ¹⁰God bless the coming kingdom of our father David! Praise be to God!"

¹¹Jesus entered Jerusalem, went into the Temple, and looked around at everything. But since it was already late in the day, he went out to Bethany with the twelve disciples.

The Second Day

The second day (11:12-19) features two events whose symbolic significance is perhaps more important than their historical substance. The cursing of the fig tree and the cleansing of the Temple comment on Israel's failure to receive the son of David when and as he came to it. The cursing of the fig tree (11:12-14) is meant to comment on the state of the Temple (11:15-19). This is clear from the fact that the story of the fig tree is interrupted and taken up again in (11:20-21).

When Jesus returned to the Temple, he found things there that apparently offended his religious ideals. The Temple area was being commercialized, and apparently part of it was being used as a shortcut.

Jesus explains his actions through quotations from Isaiah 56:7 and Jeremiah 7:11. The verse from Jeremiah is particularly appropriate, since ,it is part of the prophet's narrative about the Temple in Jerusalem and a previous generation of hypocrites.

The reaction of the chief priests and the scribes in 11:18 marks an ominous turning point.

Jesus Curses the Fig Tree
(Also Matt. 21.18—19)

¹²The next day, as they were coming back from Bethany, Jesus was hungry. ¹³He saw in the distance a fig tree covered with leaves, so he went to it to see if he could find any figs on it; but when he came to it he found only leaves because it was not the right time for figs. ¹⁴Jesus said to the fig tree: "No one shall ever eat figs from you again!" And his disciples heard him.

¹⁵When they arrived in Jerusalem, Jesus went to the Temple and began to drive out all those who bought and sold in the Temple. He overturned the tables of the money-changers and the stools of those who sold pigeons, ¹⁶and would not let anyone carry anything through the Temple courts. ¹⁷He then taught the people, "It is written in the Scriptures that God said, 'My house will be called a house of prayer for all peoples.' But you have turned it into a hideout for thieves!"

¹⁸The chief priests and the teachers of the Law heard of this, so they began looking for some way to kill Jesus. They were afraid of him, because the whole crowd was amazed at his teaching.

¹⁹When evening came, Jesus and his disciples left the city.

The Third Day

The third day (11:20—13:37) begins by taking up the story of the fig tree in 11:20-21. Attached to the cursing of the fig tree and the cleansing of the Temple are teachings on the power of prayer. The key words in the three teachings on prayer are faith and prayer. The introductory admonition in 11:22 provides the context for the teachings.

The story of the fig tree reinforces the idea of Jesus' power over nature and authority to teach. Here Jesus proclaims that the success of prayer depends on faith.

The third teaching on prayer (11:25) concerns the duty to forgive others as the necessary predisposition for prayer. This section on prayer echoes the Lord's Prayer in many respects. The reliance upon, or faith in God's power to do all things, and the notion of the reciprocity of forgiveness are two examples.

The Lesson from the Fig Tree
(Also Matt. 21.20–22)

[20]Early next morning, as they walked along the road, they saw the fig tree. It was dead all the way down to its roots. [21]Peter remembered what had happened and said to Jesus, "Look, Teacher, the fig tree you cursed has died!" [22]Jesus answered them: "Remember this! If you have faith in God, [23]you can say to this hill, 'Get up and throw yourself in the sea.' If you do not doubt in your heart, but believe that what you say will happen, it will be done for you. [24]For this reason I tell you: When you pray and ask for something, believe that you have received it, and everything will be given you. [25]And when you stand praying, forgive whatever you have against anyone, so that your Father in heaven will forgive your sins. [[26]If you do not forgive others, neither will your Father in heaven forgive your sins.]"

Jesus and His Opponents

A large part of the third day is devoted to controversies between Jesus and his opponents in Jerusalem (11:27–12:37). In many respects these stories are like the controversies in Galilee that were the subject of 2:1–3:6. Most of them begin by describing a situation of conflict between Jesus and his rivals. The opponents put Jesus on the spot or try to trap him by asking his opinion of a difficult problem. Jesus manages to avoid their traps either by reducing the opponents to silence or answering them in a brilliant and conclusive way. The opponents are embarrassed and Jesus is revealed as a marvelously clever teacher. These conflict stories were treasured in the early Christian communities and handed on from group to group. Mark used them in order to develop the atmosphere of controversy and hostility that resulted in Jesus' arrest and death in Jerusalem. Instead of recognizing and accepting the authoritative teachings of Jesus, the opponents grow more jealous and bolder in their efforts at destroying Jesus.

The first controversy (11:27-33) involves the source of Jesus' authority. The questioners want to know by what authority Jesus does "these things," most likely a reference to his cleansing of the Temple. Jesus answers his opponents by asking them another question in 11:30. The device of the counter-question was often used by Jewish teachers of Jesus' time. Here Jesus confounds his opponents by presenting them with a dilemma. Admitting that John's right to baptize came from God would be an admission to the authority of Jesus, since John proclaimed Jesus to be greater than himself.

■ *Reflection*
Are there any dilemmas which challenge the Christian message today? How can they be stated?

²⁷So they came back to Jerusalem. As Jesus was walking in the Temple, the chief priests, the teachers of the Law, and the elders came to him ²⁸and asked him: "What right do you have to do these things? Who gave you the right to do them?" ²⁹Jesus answered them: "I will ask you just one question, and if you give me an answer I will tell you what right I have to do these things. ³⁰Tell me, where did John's right to baptize come from; from God or from man?" ³¹They started to argue among themselves: "What shall we say? If we answer, 'From God,' he will say, 'Why, then, did you not believe John?' ³²But if we say, 'From man . . .'" (They were afraid of the people, because everyone was convinced that John had been a prophet.) ³³So their answer to Jesus was, "We don't know." And Jesus said to them, "Neither will I tell you, then, by what right I do these things."

The Vineyard

The series of five controversies is interrupted by the parable of the vineyard in 12:1-12. The parable in its present context shows that Jesus' suffering and death stood in line with the fate of the prophets before him. At the same time Mark suggests that the identity of Jesus is different from the prophets. He is the son of the owner of the vineyard. He has a right to expect better treatment, yet his fate is the same.

The action of the owner described in 11:9 was understood in early Christian circles as fulfilled in the Roman destruction of Jerusalem in A.D. 70 (see Matthew 21:41, 43; 22:7; Luke 19:43-44; 21:20, 24).

The Parable of the Tenants in the Vineyard
(Also Matt. 21.33–46; Luke 20.9–19)

12 Then Jesus spoke to them in parables: "There was a man who planted a vineyard, put a fence around it, dug a hole for the winepress, and built a watchtower. Then he rented the vineyard to tenants and left home on a trip. ²When the time came for gathering the grapes, he sent a slave to the tenants to receive from them his share of the harvest. ³The tenants grabbed the slave, beat him and sent him back without a thing. ⁴Then the owner sent another slave; the tenants beat him over the head and treated him shamefully. ⁵The owner sent another slave, and they killed him; and they treated many others the same way, beating some and killing others. ⁶The only one left to send was the man's own dear son. Last of all, then, he sent his son to the tenants. 'I am sure they will respect my son,' he said. ⁷But those tenants said to one another, 'This is the owner's son. Come on, let us kill him, and the vineyard will be ours!'' ⁸So they took the son and killed him, and threw his body out of the vineyard.

⁹"What, then, will the owner of the vineyard do?" asked Jesus. "He will come and kill those men and turn over the vineyard to other tenants. ¹⁰Surely you have read this scripture?

'The stone which the builders rejected
  as worthless
Turned out to be the most important
  stone.
¹¹This was done by the Lord,
How wonderful it is!' ''

¹²The Jewish leaders tried to arrest Jesus, because they knew that he had told this parable against them. They were afraid of the crowd, however, so they left him and went away.

Taxes to Caesar

The second controversy story (12:13-17) concerns the obligation to pay taxes to the Roman government. Palestine had been part of the Roman empire for many years, and the imposition of taxes on the Jews had been the occasion of several uprisings. The Jerusalem officials sent Pharisees and Herodians to inquire about Jesus' opinion on the matter of paying taxes to Rome.

The early Church's attitude toward the Roman empire is reflected to a large extent in this Gospel incident. Read Romans 13:1-7 and 1 Peter 2:13-17. There need not be a conflict between being a good Christian and being a good citizen of the Roman empire, as long as the empire did not encroach on "what belongs to God" (12:17).

The Question About Paying Taxes
(Also Matt. 22.15–22; Luke 20.20–26)

¹³Some Pharisees and some members of Herod's party were sent to Jesus to trap him with questions. ¹⁴They came to him and said: "Teacher, we know that you are an honest man. You don't worry about what people think, because you pay no attention to what a man seems to be, but you teach the truth about God's will for man. Tell us, is it against our Law to pay taxes to the Roman Emperor? Should we pay them, or not?" ¹⁵But Jesus saw through their trick and answered: "Why are

you trying to trap me? Bring a silver coin, and let me see it." [16]They brought him one and he asked, "Whose face and name are these?" "The Emperor's," they answered. [17]So Jesus said, "Well, then, pay to the Emperor what belongs to him, and pay to God what belongs to God." And they were filled with wonder at him.

The Resurrection of the Dead

The third controversy (12:18-27) concerns the general resurrection of the dead at the end of time. The questioners in this controversy are the Sadducees, members of a conservative and aristocratic group that recognized only the first five books of the Old Testament (the Pentateuch) as authoritative. Since the most important references to the resurrection occur in other books of the Old Testament (see Daniel 12:2; Isaiah 26:19; Psalm 73:23-24), the Sadducees rejected the resurrection of the dead as an article of faith.

The Sadducees knew that Jesus agreed with the Pharisees that there will be a general resurrection at the end of time, and so they devised a case that they thought would reveal belief in the resurrection to be foolish and contrary to Scripture.

In Genesis 38:8 and Deuteronomy 25:5 it is clear that the concern in the Old Testament law is for the continuance of the line of descendants of the older brother. The law was not addressed to the question of resurrection, only to the kind of immortality that is gained in future generations of one's family.

Jesus responds to the Sadducees by showing that they know nothing about the Scripture or about the power of God. By quoting from Exodus 3:6, Jesus was using a source that the Sadducees believed to be authoritative.

[18]Some Sadducees came to Jesus. (They are the ones who say that people will not be raised from death.) [19]"Teacher," they said, "Moses wrote this law for us: 'If a man dies and leaves a wife, but no children, that man's brother must marry the widow so they can have children for the dead man.' [20]Once there were seven brothers; the oldest got married, and died without having children. [21]Then the next one married the widow and he died without having children. The same thing happened to the third brother, [22]and then to the rest; all seven brothers married the woman and died without having children. Last of all, the woman died. [23]Now, when all the dead are risen to life on the day of resurrection, whose wife will she be? All seven of them had married her!"

[24]Jesus answered them: "How wrong you are! And do you know why? It is because you don't know the Scriptures or God's power. [25]For when the dead are raised to life they will be like the angels in heaven, and men and women will not marry. [26]Now, about the dead being raised: haven't you ever read in the book of Moses the passage about the burning bush? For there it is written that God said to Moses, 'I am the God of Abraham, the God of Isaac, and the God of Jacob.' [27]That means that he is the God of the living, not of the dead. You are completely wrong!"

Two More Disputes

The fourth controversy (12:28-34) involves the most important commandment of the Old Testament. The questioner in this story was a scribe, someone skilled in interpreting and applying the laws of the Old Testament. Like other Jewish teachers of his time, Jesus was asked to summarize the Old Testament law. His summary consists of quotations from Deuteronomy 6:4-5 and Leviticus 19:18. Since Deuteronomy 6:4-5 was part of the Jewish daily prayer, the scribe could not disagree with Jesus' position. The second part of Jesus' answer (Leviticus 19:18) insists on showing the same concern for others that we so naturally and instinctively show ourselves.

The fifth and final controversy (12:35-37) in the series involves the interpretation of Psalm 110:1. Jesus' point is not to deny that the Messiah is David's son, but rather to suggest that a higher view of the Messiah's origin and mission is necessary: as Lord, he is more than David's son.

As a concluding comment on the five controversies, a contrast is drawn between the hypocrisy of the scribes (12:38-40) and the unpretentious piety of the poor widow (12:41-44).

The Great Commandment
(Also Matt. 22.34—40; Luke 10.25—28)

[28]A teacher of the Law was there who heard the discussion. He saw that Jesus had given the Sadducees a good answer, so he came to him with a question: "Which commandment is the most important of all?" [29]"This is the most important one," said Jesus. " 'Hear, Israel! The Lord our God is the only Lord. [30]You must love the Lord your God with all your heart, and with all your soul, and will all your mind, and with all your strength.' [31]The second most important commandment is this: 'You must love your neighbor as yourself.' There is no other commandment more important than these

two." ³²The teacher of the Law said to Jesus: "Well done, Teacher! It is true, as you say, that only the Lord is God, and that there is no other god but he. ³³And so man must love God with all his heart, and with all his mind, and with all his strength; and he must love his neighbor as himself. It is much better to obey these two commandments than to bring animals to be burned on the altar and offer other sacrifices to God." ³⁴Jesus noticed how wise his answer was, and so he told him: "You are not far from the Kingdom of God." After this nobody dared to ask Jesus any more questions.

The Question About the Messiah
(Also Matt. 22.41–46; Luke 20.41–44)

³⁵As Jesus was teaching in the Temple he asked the question: "How can the teachers of the Law say that the Messiah will be the descendant of David? ³⁶The Holy Spirit inspired David to say:

'The Lord said to my Lord:
Sit here at my right side,
Until I put your enemies under your feet.'

³⁷David himself called him 'Lord': how, then, can the Messiah be David's descendant?"

Jesus Warns Against the Teachers of the Law
(Also Matt. 23.1–36; Luke 20.45–47)

The large crowd heard Jesus gladly. ³⁸As he taught them he said: "Watch out for the teachers of the Law, who like to walk around in their long robes and be greeted with respect in the marketplace; ³⁹who choose the reserved seats in the synagogues and the best places at feasts. ⁴⁰They take advantage of widows and rob them of their homes, then make a show of saying long prayers! Their punishment will be all the worse!"

⁴¹As Jesus sat near the Temple treasury he watched the people as they dropped in their money. Many rich men dropped in much money; ⁴²then a poor widow came along and dropped in two little copper coins, worth about a penny. ⁴³He called his disciples together and said to them: "I tell you that this poor widow put more in the offering box than all the others. ⁴⁴For the others put in what they had to spare of their riches; but she, poor as she is, put in all she had—she gave all she had to live on."

The End of the World

The second major block of Jesus' teaching on the third day is his discourse about the future in chapter 13. There is a wide agreement that this chapter contains some genuine sayings of Jesus and some material taken from a Jewish or Jewish-Christian writing (see 13:7-8, 14-20, 24-27). Rather than arguing about which material is original with Jesus and which belongs to the source, attention should be drawn to the place of the discourse in its present form within the Gospel as a whole.

The first part of Jesus' answer (13:5-13) goes beyond the disciples' question about the destruction of the Jerusalem Temple and describes the "beginning of the sufferings" (13:8) that will eventually lead to the end of the world as we know it.

The material in 13:9-13 would have had a special relevance for early Christians who were experiencing persecution or expected it soon. There was a belief that the second coming would occur in their generation. The more widespread the good news was preached, the closer the world was to the final coming of the kingdom. Thus preaching and patience in suffering were both emphasized by the Gospel writers.

The second part of Jesus' teaching (13:14-23) describes the great tribulation and the events surrounding it. The desolating sacrilege or abomination of desolation in 13:14 originally referred to Antiochus IV Epiphanes' placing an altar dedicated to Olympian Zeus in the Jerusalem Temple in 167 B.C. (see Daniel 11:31; 12:11; 1 Maccabees 1:54). The parenthetical comment in 13:14 ("Note to the reader: understand what this means!") suggests that the term is being transferred to some greater and still future horror.

The third and climatic part of the discourse (13:24-27) describes the future coming of the Son of Man. The parallel Old Testament text is the vision of Daniel 7:13. Jesus identifies himself as the Lord coming in glory at the end of the world.

The final part of the discourse (13:28-37) stresses confidence and watchfulness. Confidence is expected because Jesus' resurrection is a promise of his power to gather God's people around him in the kingdom, a kingdom that may be established within the time of his generation. Watchfulness is necessary because only the Father knows the time of the coming of the Son of Man.

■ *Reflection*
What effect should predictions of the end of the world have on our lives as Christians?

Jesus Speaks of the Destruction of the Temple
(Also Matt. 24.1–2; Luke 21.5–6)

13 As Jesus was leaving the Temple, one of his disciples said, "Look, Teacher! What wonderful stones and buildings!" ²Jesus answered: "You see these great buildings? Not a single stone here will be left in its place; every one of them will be thrown down."

³Jesus was sitting on the Mount of Olives, across from the Temple, when Peter, James, John, and Andrew came to him in private. ⁴"Tell us when this will be," they said; "and tell us what is the sign that will show that it is the time for all these things to happen."

⁵Jesus began to teach them: "Watch out, and don't let anyone fool you. ⁶Many men will come in my name, saying, 'I am he!' and fool many people. ⁷And don't be troubled when you hear the noise of battles close by and news of battles far away. Such things must happen, but they do not mean that the end has come. ⁸One country will fight another country, one kingdom will attack another kingdom. There will be earthquakes everywhere, and there will be famines. These things are like the first pains of childbirth.

⁹"You yourselves must watch out. For men will arrest you and take you to court. You will be beaten in the synagogues; you will stand before rulers and kings for my sake, to tell them the Good News. ¹⁰The gospel must first be preached to all peoples. ¹¹And when they arrest you and take you to court, do not worry ahead of time about what you are going to say; when the time comes, say whatever is given to you then. For the words you speak will not be

yours; they will come from the Holy Spirit. [12]Men will hand over their own brothers to be put to death, and fathers will do the same to their children; children will turn against their parents and have them put to death. [13]Everyone will hate you because of me. But the person who holds out to the end will be saved."

The Awful Horror
(Also Matt. 24.15–28; Luke 21.20–24)

[14]"You will see 'The Awful Horror' standing in the place where he should not be." (Note to the reader: understand what this means!) "Then those who are in Judea must run away to the hills. [15]The man who is on the roof of his house must not lose time by going down into the house to get anything to take with him. [16]The man who is in the field must not go back to the house for his cloak. [17]How terrible it will be in those days for women who are pregnant, and for mothers who have little babies! [18]Pray to God that these things will not happen in wintertime! [19]For the trouble of those days will be far worse than any the world has ever known, from the very beginning when God created the world until the present time. Nor will there ever again be anything like it. [20]But the Lord has reduced the number of those days; if he had not, nobody would survive. For the sake of his chosen people, however, he has reduced those days.

[21]"Then, if anyone says to you, 'Look, here is the Messiah!' or, 'Look, there he is!'—do not believe him. [22]For false Messiahs and false prophets will appear. They will perform signs and wonders for the purpose of deceiving God's chosen people, if possible. [23]Be on your guard! I have told you everything ahead of time."

The Coming of the Son of Man
(Also Matt. 24.29–31; Luke 21.25–28)

²⁴"In the days after that time of trouble the sun will grow dark, the moon will no longer shine, ²⁵the stars will fall from heaven, and the powers in space will be driven from their course. ²⁶Then the Son of Man will appear, coming in the clouds with great power and glory. ²⁷He will send out the angels to the four corners of the earth and gather God's chosen people from one end of the world to the other."

The Lesson of the Fig Tree
(Also Matt. 24.32–35; Luke 21.29–33)

²⁸"Let the fig tree teach you a lesson. When its branches become green and tender, and it starts putting out leaves, you know that summer is near. ²⁹In the same way, when you see these things happening, you will know that the time is near, ready to begin. ³⁰Remember this! All these things will happen before the people now living have all died. ³¹Heaven and earth will pass away; my words will never pass away."

No One Knows the Day or Hour
(Also Matt. 24.36–44)

³²"No one knows, however, when that day or hour will come—neither the angels in heaven, nor the Son; only the Father knows. ³³Be on watch, be alert, for you do not know when the time will be. ³⁴It will be like a man who goes away from home on a trip and leaves his servants in charge, each one with his own work to do; and he tells the doorkeeper to keep watch. ³⁵Watch, then, because you do not know

when the master of the house is coming—it might be in the evening, or at midnight, or before dawn, or at sunrise. ³⁶If he comes suddenly, he must not find you asleep! ³⁷What I say to you, then, I say to all: Watch!''

■ Discussion

1. How is Jesus' identity brought out in the events of the first day?

2. How is Israel's need for repentance brought out in the events of the second day?

3. How is Jesus' skill as a religious teacher brought out on the third day?

4. What style of piety and prayer does Jesus recommend in Mark's Gospel?

5. Can we learn anything definite about the end of the world from this Gospel account? What attitudes toward the end of the world does Jesus recommend?

■ Prayer and Meditation

"The stone which the builders rejected as worthless
   turned out to be the most important of all.
This was done by the LORD;
   what a wonderful sight it is!
This is the day of the LORD'S victory;
   let us be happy, let us celebrate!
Save us, LORD, save us!
 • Give us success, O LORD!

May God bless the one who comes in the name of the
   LORD!
From the Temple of the LORD we bless you.
The LORD is God; he has been good to us.
With branches in your hands, start the festival
   and march around the altar.

You are my God, and I give you thanks;
   I will proclaim your greatness.

Give thanks to the LORD, because he is good,
   and his love is eternal."

                                        Psalm 118:22–29

Jesus' Death in Jerusalem ___ Mark 14:1—16:8

Mark's Gospel is sometimes described as a passion narrative with a long introduction. Although that description may be an overstatement, it does make clear the importance of Jesus' suffering, death and resurrection in this Gospel. Many features in the first thirteen chapters—the growing hostility among the groups opposed to Jesus, the commands by Jesus for others to be silent about his true identity, the cosmic struggle between good and evil, the misunderstanding on the part of the disciples—have prepared for the climactic events in Jerusalem. There the opponents will gain an apparent victory over Jesus by having him arrested and executed as a criminal. There the true identity of Jesus will be revealed in his atoning death and ultimate triumph over death. There the cosmic struggle between good and evil will enter a decisive phase. There the disciples come to learn that Jesus is not only a wonder-worker and a teacher, but also the suffering righteous one and the Son of God.

Preparation for Burial

The passion narrative begins with the familiar Markan technique of sandwiching the report about the plot to arrest Jesus and the story of the anointing at Bethany. These events occur in the spring. Passover was the celebration of Israel's escape from Egypt under the leadership of Moses, and Unleavened Bread was the old agricultural festival of spring. They were two names for one eight-day observance during which many Jews made a pilgrimage to Jerusalem.

Meanwhile in a small village outside of Jerusalem, a woman performs for Jesus a cermonial act of hospitality and respect by anointing him (14:3-9). John 12:1-8 identifies the woman as Mary, sister of Lazarus. The anointing has a double symbolism. First it indicates a preparation for burial, a preparation for which there was no time after Jesus' death. It was to anoint Jesus that the women went to the tomb on Easter morning. The second symbolism is that of Jesus' identity, the anointed one, the Christ, the Messiah.

The story of the plot against Jesus is resumed in 14:10-11. The sandwich technique allows Mark to point up the contrast between the treachery of Judas and the piety of the woman who anointed Jesus.

The Plot Against Jesus
(Also Matt. 26.1–5; Luke 22.1–2; John 11.45–53)

14 It was now two days before the Feast of Passover and Unleavened Bread. The chief priests and teachers of the Law were looking for a way to arrest Jesus secretly and put him to death. ²"We must not do it during the feast," they said, "or the people might riot."

³Jesus was in the house of Simon the leper, in Bethany; while he was eating, a woman came in with an alabaster jar full of a very expensive perfume, made of pure nard. She broke the jar and poured the perfume on Jesus' head. ⁴Some of the people there became angry, and said to each other, "What was the use of wasting the perfume? ⁵It could have been sold for

more than three hundred dollars, and the money given to the poor!'' And they criticized her harshly. ⁶But Jesus said: "Leave her alone! Why are you bothering her? She has done a fine and beautiful thing for me. ⁷You will always have poor people with you, and any time you want to you can help them. But I shall not be with you always. ⁸She did what she could: she poured perfume on my body to prepare it for burial ahead of time. ⁹Now, remember this! Wherever the gospel is preached, all over the world, what she has done will be told in memory of her.''

Judas Agrees to Betray Jesus
(Also Matt. 26.14—16; Luke 22.3—6)

¹⁰ Then Judas Iscariot, one of the twelve disciples, went off to the chief priests in order to hand Jesus over to them. ¹¹They were greatly pleased to hear what he had to say, and promised to give him money. So Judas started looking for a good chance to betray Jesus.

The Passover Meal

The celebration of Passover begins at sundown after the sacrifice of the lamb at the Temple in Jerusalem. Jesus' instructions to the disciples about the preparations for their Passover meal (14:12-16) may reflect an arrangement already made with the householder, or it may indicate Jesus' foreknowledge of the events of the passion. There is a long historical debate over whether the Last Supper actually took place on the first evening of the Passover or on the day before it (see John 13:1; 18:28). In either case, the story of Jesus is placed firmly in the context of the Passover season.

The account of the Last Supper (14:17-31) sand-wiches passages about Jesus' foreknowledge that his disciples would betray him around the institution of the Eucharist. Thus Jesus' self-giving is contrasted with the treachery of his closest followers.

At the supper Jesus performs actions that would have been familiar to Jews from their Sabbath and festival meals, but he uses these actions to bring out the real meaning of his death. The sharing of the bread and the cup are for Mark an invitation to the disciples from Jesus to share in his death.

Jesus' foreknowledge and the disciples' treachery are emphasized once more in the prophecy of Peter's denial (14:26-31). The effect that Jesus' death will have on his followers is described in 14:27 with words taken from Zechariah 13:7. But after his resurrection Jesus will go to Galilee and be with his disciples again (see 16:7).

■ *Reflection*
Is the celebration of the Eucharist as we experience it today faithful to the intent of Jesus at the Last Supper?

Jesus Eats the Passover Meal with His Disciples
(Also Matt. 26.17–25; Luke 22.7–14, 21–23; John 13.21–30)

¹²On the first day of the Feast of Unleavened Bread, the day the lambs for the Passover meal were killed, Jesus' disciples asked him: "Where do you want us to go and get your Passover supper ready?" ¹³Then Jesus sent two of them out with these instructions: "Go into the city, and a man carrying a jar of water will meet you. ¹⁴Follow him to the house he enters, and say to the owner of the house: 'The

Teacher says, Where is my room where my disciples and I shall eat the Passover supper?' ¹⁵Then he will show you a large upstairs room, fixed up and furnished, where you will get things ready for us." ¹⁶The disciples left, went to the city, and found everything just as Jesus had told them; and they prepared the Passover supper.

¹⁷When it was evening, Jesus came with the twelve disciples. ¹⁸While they were at the table eating, Jesus said: "I tell you this: one of you will betray me—one who is eating with me." ¹⁹The disciples were upset and began to ask him, one after the other, "Surely you don't mean me, do you?" ²⁰Jesus answered: "It will be one of you twelve, one who dips his bread in the dish with me. ²¹The Son of Man will die as the Scriptures say he will; but how terrible for that man who will betray the Son of Man! It would have been better for that man if he had never been born!"

The Lord's Supper
(Also Matt. 26.26–30; Luke 22.15–20; 1 Cor. 11.23–25)

²²While they were eating, Jesus took the bread, gave a prayer of thanks, broke it, and gave it to his disciples. "Take it," he said, "this is my body." ²³Then he took the cup, gave thanks to God, and handed it to them; and they all drank from it. ²⁴Jesus said: "This is my blood which is poured out for many, my blood which seals God's covenant. ²⁵I tell you, I will never again drink this wine until the day I drink the new wine in the Kingdom of God." ²⁶Then they sang a hymn and went out to the Mount of Olives.

²⁷Jesus said to them: "All of you will run away and leave me, for the scripture says, 'God will kill the shepherd and the sheep will all be scattered.' ²⁸But after I am raised to life I will go to Galilee ahead of you." ²⁹Peter answered, "I will never leave you, even though all the rest do!" ³⁰"Remember this!" Jesus said to Peter. "Before the rooster crows two times tonight, you will say three times that you do not know me." ³¹Peter answered even more strongly: "I will never say I do not know you, even if I have to die with you!" And all the disciples said the same thing.

The Weakness of the Disciples

Accompanied by the inner circle of his disciples, Jesus prays in Gethsemane (14:32-42), which was a small garden on the Mount of Olives, outside the eastern wall of Jerusalem. The character of Jesus is contrasted with that of the disciples. Jesus' acceptance of suffering is a model for Christians. The disciples' attitude is a negative example.

We see here again echoes of the Lord's Prayer, ". . . not what I want, but what you want." Mark encourages Christians of his day to identify with the suffering of Jesus.

The story of Jesus' arrest (14:43-52) develops the treacherous character of Judas, insists that Jesus was not a criminal or a revolutionary, and shows how these events took place in accordance with God's will.

The behavior of the disciples is in marked contrast to Jesus' acceptance of God's will. The flight of the young man (14:51-52) is a dramatization of the general flight of the disciples. They could not grasp the necessity and importance of Jesus' passion.

Jesus in Gethsemane
(Also Matt. 26.36–46; Luke 22.39–46)

³²They came to a place called Gethsemane, and Jesus said to his disciples, "Sit here while I pray." ³³Then he took Peter, James, and John with him. Distress and anguish came over him, ³⁴and he said to them: "The sorrow in my heart is so great that it almost crushes me. Stay here and watch." ³⁵He went a little farther on, threw himself on the ground and prayed that, if possible, he might not have to go through the hour of suffering. ³⁶"Father!" he prayed, "my Father! All things are possible for you. Take this cup away from me. But not what I want, but what you want."

³⁷Then he returned and found the three disciples asleep, and said to Peter, "Simon, are you asleep? Weren't you able to stay awake for one hour?" ³⁸And he said to them, "Keep watch, and pray, so you will not fall into temptation. The spirit is willing, but the flesh is weak."

³⁹He went away once more and prayed, saying the same words. ⁴⁰Then he came back to the disciples and found them asleep; they could not keep their eyes open. And they did not know what to say to him.

⁴¹When he came back the third time, he said to them: "Are you still sleeping and resting? Enough! The hour has come! Look, the Son of Man is now handed over to the power of sinful men. ⁴²Rise, let us go. Look, here is the man who is betraying me!"

⁴³He was still talking when Judas, one of the twelve disciples, arrived. A crowd carrying swords and clubs was with him, sent by the chief priests, the teachers of the Law, and the elders. ⁴⁴The traitor had given the crowd a signal: "The man I kiss is the one you want. Arrest him and take him away under guard."

⁴⁵As soon as Judas arrived he went up to Jesus and said, "Teacher!" and kissed him. ⁴⁶So they arrested Jesus and held him tight. ⁴⁷But one of those standing by drew his sword and struck at the High Priest's slave, cutting off his ear. ⁴⁸Then Jesus spoke up and said to them: "Did you have to come with swords and clubs to capture me, as though I were an outlaw? ⁴⁹Day after day I was with you teaching in the Temple, and you did not arrest me. But the Scriptures must come true." ⁵⁰Then all the disciples left him and ran away.

⁵¹A certain young man, dressed only in a linen cloth, was following Jesus. They tried to arrest him, ⁵²but he ran away naked, leaving the linen cloth behind.

Trials and Conviction

The account of Jesus' trial before the high priest and the council (14:53-65) indicates that Jesus was charged with threatening to destroy the Temple (14:58) and claiming to be the Messiah (14:61-62). There are historical problems connected with the time of the proceeding (the unlikelihood of trial at night, on the first evening of the Passover), and its nature (perhaps a preliminary investigation only). But Mark (or his source) did understand it as a legal trial held at the house of the high priest after Passover had begun.

The first charge is Jesus' threat to destroy the Temple and build another in three days. Perhaps his prophetic cleansing of the Temple gave rise to this charge. Jesus' opponents would be upset by any hint of destroying the Temple for religious, economic, and political reasons.

The second charge concerns Jesus' identity and provides the grounds for condemning him to death. Jesus' admission that he is the Messiah and the Son of God does not seem to merit the description of blasphemy (cursing God) as it is specified in Leviticus 24:10-23. Jesus' statement, however, indicates that he now wishes everyone to know what previously he had asked to be kept secret. He is not just another claiming to be the Messiah; he is the Son of God.

The story of Peter's denial of Jesus (14:66-72) began in 14:54, and so it is at least a semi-sandwich. Peter's unfaithfulness contrasts sharply with Jesus' faithfulness until death. Although Peter is presented in a very negative way in this episode, his bad example would also have given encouragement to early Christians in their own failures. The story is told with great drama. With each denial the audience grows, and Peter becomes more vehement until he finally realizes what he has done.

In his trial before Pilate (15:1-15), the responsiblity of the Jewish leaders for Jesus' death is emphasized and even heightened. Pontius Pilate was the military governor of Judea from A.D. 26 to 36. He had his headquarters at Caesarea on the Mediterranean coast, but came to Jerusalem to keep the peace during the Passover pilgrimage. The indecisiveness and concern for justice attributed to him in the Gospels contradict other ancient descriptions of his obstinacy and cruelty.

The practice of pardoning a Jewish prisoner every year at Passover time (15:6-7) is not otherwise reported in ancient sources outside the New Testament. According to the Gospel, the crowd in Jerusalem was asked to choose between the murdering revolutionary Barabbas and the innocent wonder-worker and teacher Jesus the Son of God. On historical grounds it is likely that Pilate bore the ultimate legal responsibility for the death of Jesus by crucifixion. The idea of cooperation between the Jewish high priest and Pilate is true to the political situation in Jerusalem at that time. Mark (or his source) probably built up the responsiblitiy of the Jewish leaders and played down Pilate's part. At any rate there is no reason at all to attribute responsibility to all the Jews of Jesus' time or to Jews of later times.

■ Reflection

How would you describe the kingship of Jesus for today's Christians?

Jesus Before the Council
(Also Matt. 26.57–68; Luke 22.54–55, 63–71; John 18.13–14, 19–24)

⁵³Then they took Jesus to the High Priest's house, where all the chief priests, the elders, and the teachers of the Law were gathering. ⁵⁴Peter followed far behind and went into the courtyard of the High Priest's house. There he sat down with the guards, keeping himself warm by the fire. ⁵⁵The chief priests and the whole Council tried to find some evidence against Jesus, in order to put him to death, but they could not find any. ⁵⁶Many witnesses told lies against Jesus, but their stories did not agree.

⁵⁷Then some men stood up and told this lie against Jesus: ⁵⁸"We heard him say, 'I will tear

down this Temple which men made, and after three days I will build one that is not made by men.' " ⁵⁹Not even they, however, could make their stories agree.

⁶⁰The High Priest stood up in front of them all and questioned Jesus: "Have you no answer to the accusation they bring against you?" ⁶¹But Jesus kept quiet and would not say a word. Again the High Priest questioned him: "Are you the Messiah, the Son of the Blessed God?" ⁶²"I am," answered Jesus, "and you will all see the Son of Man seated at the right side of the Almighty, and coming with the clouds of heaven!" ⁶³The High Priest tore his robes and said, "We don't need any more witnesses! ⁶⁴You heard his wicked words. What is your decision?" They all voted against him: he was guilty and should be put to death.

⁶⁵Some of them began to spit on Jesus, and they blindfolded him and hit him. "Guess who hit you!" they said. And the guards took him and slapped him.

Peter Denies Jesus
(Also Matt. 26.69–75; Luke 22.56–62; John 18.15–18, 25–27)

⁶⁶Peter was still down in the courtyard when one of the High Priest's servant girls came by. ⁶⁷When she saw Peter warming himself, she looked straight at him and said, "You, too, were with Jesus of Nazareth." ⁶⁸But he denied it. "I don't know ... I don't understand what you are talking about," he answered, and went out into the passageway. Just then a rooster crowed. ⁶⁹The servant girl saw him there and began to repeat to the bystanders, "He is one of them!" ⁷⁰But Peter denied it again. A little while later the bystanders accused Peter

again: "You can't deny that you are one of them, because you, too, are from Galilee." [71]Then Peter made a vow: "May God punish me if I am not telling the truth! I do not know the man you are talking about!" [72]Just then a rooster crowed a second time, and Peter remembered how Jesus had said to him, "Before the rooster crows two times you will say three times that you do not know me." And he broke down and cried.

15 Early in the morning the chief priests met hurriedly with the elders, the teachers of the Law, and the whole Council, and made their plans. They put Jesus in chains, took him away and handed him over to Pilate. [2]Pilate questioned him: "Are you the king of the Jews?" Jesus answered: "So you say." [3]The chief priests accused Jesus of many things, [4]so Pilate questioned him again: "Aren't you going to answer? See how many things they accuse you of!" [5]Again Jesus refused to say a word, and Pilate was filled with surprise.

Jesus Is Sentenced to Death
(Also Matt. 27.15–26; Luke 23.13–25; John 18.39–19.16)

[6]At every Passover Feast Pilate would set free any prisoner the people asked for. [7]At that time a man named Barabbas was in prison with the rebels who had committed murder in the riot. [8]When the crowd gathered and began to ask Pilate to do them the usual favor, [9]Pilate asked them: "Do you want me to set free for you the king of the Jews?" [10]He knew very well that the chief priests had handed Jesus over to him because they were jealous. [11]But the chief priests stirred up the crowd to ask, instead, for

Pilate to set Barabbas free for them. [12]Pilate spoke again to the crowd: "What then, do you want me to do with the one you call the king of the Jews?" [13]They shouted back, "Nail him to the cross!" [14]"But what crime has he committed?" Pilate asked. They shouted all the louder, "Nail him to the cross!" [15]Pilate wanted to please the crowd, so he set Barabbas free for them. Then he had Jesus whipped and handed him over to be nailed to the cross.

Death on the Cross

The account of the mockery of Jesus (15:16-20) tells how the soldiers stationed in Jerusalem unwittingly acknowledge the kingship of Jesus.

The story of Jesus' crucifixion (15:21-32) conveys a large amount of information, but it also emphasizes how Jesus' death took place in accord with the Scriptures and how Jesus was utterly abandoned in death. Little emphasis is laid on the terrible character of Jesus' physical sufferings.

Simon of Cyrene (in North Africa) was forced to carry the crossbeam to the place of execution just ouside the walls of Jerusalem. At the site of the execution Jesus refuses the offer of drugged wine (see Proverbs 31:6-7) intended to ease his sufferings. His garments are taken by the soldiers overseeing the execution and made the prize in a game of chance.

The skeletal remains of a crucified man have been discovered recently outside of Jerusalem, and careful study of those remains has resulted in the following description of the process of crucifixion: "The feet were joined almost parallel, both transfixed by the same nail at the heels, with the legs adjacent; the knees were doubled, the right one overlapping the left; the trunk was contorted; the upper limbs were stretched out, each stabbed by a nail in the forearm" [N. Haas, *Israel Exploration Journal* 20 (1970) 38-52].

The crucifixion account shows the influence of Psalm 22, the psalm of the righteous sufferer who is finally vindicated by God. Read Psalm 22 and compare the following texts: the division of the garments (Psalm 22:18 and Mark 15:24), the mode of crucifixion (Psalm 22:16 and Mark 15:25), the criminals crucified with Jesus (Psalm 22:16 and Mark 15:27), and the scorn heaped on Jesus by the bystanders (Psalm 22:7-8 and Mark 15:29).

According to 15:25, 34, Jesus was on the cross from 9:00 A.M. to 3:00 P.M. (compare John 19:14) and there was a period of darkness from noon to 3:00 P.M. (see Amos 8:9). Jesus' last words in 15:34 are a direct quotation from Psalm 22:1.

The actual death of Jesus on the cross is narrated in 15:37 with great simplicity. In response to it there are two important events that help us to grasp its significance: the tearing of the curtain in the Temple (15:38) and the centurion's confession that Jesus is the Son of God (15:39).

The tearing of the curtain in the Temple is taken to mean that after Jesus' death God is to be encountered directly, not through the mediation of the Temple as was the case in the Old Testament.

The centurion's confession marks the climax of the Gospel. Mark begins his account by stating that Jesus is the Son of God. This fact is proclaimed in the end by a bystander, a gentile, a symbol of all those for whom the Gospel is intended.

The Soldiers Make Fun of Jesus
(Also Matt. 27.27–31; John 19.2–3)

¹⁶The soldiers took Jesus inside the courtyard (that is, of the Governor's palace) and called together the rest of the company. ¹⁷They put a purple robe on Jesus, made a crown out of thorny branches, and put it on his head. ¹⁸Then they began to salute him: "Long live the King of the Jews!" ¹⁹And they beat him over the head with a stick, spat on him, fell on their knees and bowed down to him. ²⁰When they had finished making fun of him, they took off the purple robe and put his own clothes back on him. Then they led him out to nail him to the cross.

Jesus Is Crucified
(Also Matt.27.32–44; Luke 23.26–43; John 19.17–27)

²¹On the way they met a man named Simon, who was coming into the city from the country, and they forced him to carry Jesus' cross. (This was Simon from Cyrene, the father of Alexander and Rufus.)

²²They brought Jesus to a place called Golgotha, which means "The Place of the Skull." ²³There they tried to give him wine mixed with a drug called myrrh, but Jesus would not drink it. ²⁴So they nailed him to the cross and divided his clothes among themselves, throwing dice to see who would get which piece of clothing. ²⁵It was nine o'clock in the morning when they nailed him to the cross. ²⁶The notice of the accusation against him was written, "The King of the Jews." ²⁷They also nailed two bandits to crosses with Jesus, one on his right and the other on his left. [²⁸In this way the scripture

came true which says: "He was included with the criminals."]

²⁹People passing by shook their heads and threw insults at Jesus: "Aha! You were going to tear down the Temple and build it up in three days! ³⁰Now come down from the cross and save yourself!" ³¹In the same way the chief priests and the teachers of the Law made fun of Jesus, saying to each other: "He saved others, but he cannot save himself! ³²Let us see the Messiah, the king of Israel, come down from the cross now, and we will believe in him!" And the two who were crucified with Jesus insulted him also.

The Death of Jesus
(Also Matt. 27.45–56; Luke 23.44–49; John 19.28–30)

³³At noon the whole country was covered with darkness, which lasted for three hours. ³⁴At three o'clock Jesus cried out with a loud shout, *Eloi, Eloi, lema sabachthani?* which means, "My God, my God, why did you abandon me?" ³⁵Some of the people who were there heard him and said, "Listen, he is calling for Elijah!" ³⁶One of them ran up with a sponge, soaked it in wine, and put it on the end of a stick. Then he held it up to Jesus' lips and said, "Wait! Let us see if Elijah is coming to bring him down from the cross!" ³⁷With a loud cry Jesus died.

³⁸The curtain hanging in the Temple was torn in two, from top to bottom. ³⁹The army officer, who was standing there in front of the cross, saw how Jesus had cried out and died. "This man was really the Son of God!" he said. ⁴⁰Some women were there, looking on from a distance. Among them were Salome, Mary

Magdalene, and Mary the mother of the younger James and of Joseph. ⁴¹They had followed Jesus while he was in Galilee and helped him. Many other women were there also, who had come to Jerusalem with him.

The Resurrection

The area encircling Jerusalem in Jesus' time has been described as a vast cemetery. Bodies were placed in large burial caves and allowed to decompose for a year. Then the bones were gathered and deposited in a small stone box called an ossuary ("bone box"). A burial cave often held the remains of several generations in a family. Joseph of Arimathea, who apparently had become a follower of Jesus, offered to bury Jesus' body in his family tomb, and made the arrangements with Pilate. The report about Jesus' burial (15:40-47) establishes that Jesus was really dead and that the women who went to the tomb on Easter Sunday did not go to the wrong place.

The story of the empty tomb (16:1-8) does not prove the resurrection of Jesus, but it does demand an explanation. The explanation given in 16:6 is that God raised Jesus from the dead. In the New Testament the resurrection of Jesus is treated primarily in terms of the appearances of the risen Lord.

But the following considerations indicate that the story of the empty tomb is also important and very early: the disciples could not have preached the resurrection of Jesus, if they could be refuted by the presence of his corpse in the tomb outside of Jerusalem; the opponents of Jesus gave various explanations of the empty tomb (see Matthew 28:11-15), but never denied that the tomb was empty; no one would have invented a story in which women were the key witnesses, since in Judaism of the day the testimony of women was not legally admissible.

Mark 16:9-20 is not part of the earliest and best Greek manuscripts of the Gospels. In fact, it seems to be a second-century summary of the resurrection appearances presented in the other three Gospels that has been added to Mark's Gospel by a later editor.

■ *Reflection*
Why is the resurrection considered to be the key event in the Gospels?

The Burial of Jesus
(Also Matt. 27.57–61; Luke 23.50–56; John 19.38–42)

[42]It was getting on toward evening when Joseph of Arimathea arrived. [43]He was a respected member of the Council, who looked for the coming of the Kingdom of God. It was Preparation day (that is, the day before the Sabbath); so Joseph went in bravely to the presence of Pilate and asked him for the body of Jesus. [44]Pilate was surprised to hear that Jesus was already dead. He called the army officer and asked him if Jesus had been dead a long time. [45]After hearing the officer's report, Pilate told Joseph he could have the body. [46]Joseph bought a linen sheet, took the body down, wrapped it in the sheet and placed it in a grave which had been dug out of rock. Then he rolled a large stone across the entrance to the grave. [47]Mary Magdalene and Mary the mother of Joseph were watching, and saw where Jesus was laid.

The Resurrection
(Also Matt. 28.1–8; Luke 24.1–12; John 20.1–10)

16 After the Sabbath day was over, Mary Magdalene, Mary the mother of James, and Salome bought spices to go and anoint the body of Jesus. ²Very early on Sunday morning, at sunrise they went to the grave. ³·⁴On the way they said to one another, "Who will roll away the stone from the entrance to the grave for us?" (It was a very large stone.) Then they looked up and saw that the stone had already been rolled back. ⁵So they entered the grave, where they saw a young man, sitting at the right, who wore a white robe—and they were filled with alarm. ⁶"Don't be alarmed," he said. "You are looking for Jesus of Nazareth, who was nailed to the cross. But he is not here—he has risen! Look, here is the place where they laid him. ⁷Now go and give this message to his disciples, including Peter: 'He is going to Galilee ahead of you; there you will see him, just as he told you.' " ⁸So they went out and ran from the grave, because fear and terror were upon them. And they said nothing to anyone, because they were afraid.

An Old Ending to the Gospel

Jesus Appears to Mary Magdalene
(Also Matt. 28.9–10; John 20.11–18)

[⁹After Jesus rose from death, early on the first day of the week, he appeared first to Mary Magdalene, from whom he had driven out seven demons. ¹⁰She went and told it to his companions. They were mourning and crying; ¹¹and when they heard her say that Jesus was alive and that she had seen him, they did not believe her.

¹²After this, Jesus appeared in a different manner to two of them while they were on their way to the country. ¹³They returned and told it to the others, but they would not believe it.

Jesus Appears to the Eleven
(Also Matt. 28.16–20; Luke 24.36–49; John 20.19–23; Acts 1.6–8)

¹⁴Last of all, Jesus appeared to the eleven disciples as they were eating. He scolded them, because they did not have faith and because they were too stubborn to believe those who had seen him alive. ¹⁵He said to them: "Go to the whole world and preach the gospel to all mankind. ¹⁶Whoever believes and is baptized will be saved; whoever does not believe will be condemned. ¹⁷Believers will be given these signs of power: they will drive out demons in my name; they will speak in strange tongues; ¹⁸if they pick up snakes or drink any poison, they will not be harmed; they will place their hands on the sick, and they will get well."

Jesus Is Taken Up to Heaven
(Also Luke 24.50–53; Acts 1.9–11)

¹⁹After the Lord Jesus had talked with them, he was taken up to heaven and sat at the right side of God. ²⁰The disciples went and preached everywhere, and the Lord worked with them and proved that their preaching was true by giving them the signs of power.]

Another Old Ending

[⁹The women went to Peter and his friends and gave them a brief account of all they had been told. ¹⁰After this, Jesus himself sent out through his disciples, from the east to the west, the sacred and ever-living message of eternal salvation.]

■ Discussion

1. Who are the prime movers in bringing about the arrest and condemnation of Jesus? What were their motives?

2. What dimensions of the Eucharist emerge from Mark's account of the Last Supper?

3. How is the kingship of Jesus developed in the passion narrative?

4. What is the meaning of the crucifixion in Mark's Gospel?

5. What different effects are gained by the two endings to Mark's Gospel?

■ Prayer and Meditation

"The scripture says, 'I spoke because I believed.' In the same spirit of faith we also speak because we believe. We know that God, who raised the Lord Jesus to life, will also raise us up with Jesus and take us, together with you, into his presence. All this is for your sake; and as God's grace reaches more and more people, they will offer to the glory of God more prayers of thanksgiving.

For this reason we never become discouraged. Even though our physical being is gradually decaying, yet our spiritual being is renewed day after day. And this small and temporary trouble we suffer will bring us a tremendous and eternal glory, much greater than the trouble. For we fix our attention, not on things that are seen, but on things that are unseen. What can be seen lasts only for a time, but what cannot be seen lasts forever."

2 Corinthians 4:13–18

Bibliography _____

GENERAL
P.J. Achtemeier, *Invitation to Mark.* Garden City, NY: Doubleday/Image, 1978.

W. Harrington, *Mark.* Wilmington, DE: Michael Glazier, Inc., 1979.

H.M. Humphrey, *A Bibliography for the Gospel of Mark, 1954–1980.* New York, NY—Toronto: Edwin Mellen Press, 1981.

R.P. Martin, *Mark: Evangelist and Theologian.* Grand Rapids, MI: Zondervan, 1973.

STUDY SESSION ONE
A.M. Ambrozic, *The Hidden Kingdom.* Washington, DC: Catholic Bible Association, 1972.

J. Dewey, *Markan Public Debate.* Chico, CA: Scholars Press, 1980.

A.J. Hultgren, *Jesus and His Adversaries.* Minneapolis, MN: Augsburg, 1979.

W. Marxsen, *Mark the Evangelist.* Nashville, TN: Abingdon, 1969.

J.M. Robinson, *The Problem of History in Mark.* London: SCM, 1957.

STUDY SESSION TWO

M. Boucher, *The Mysterious Parable.* Washington, DC: Catholic Biblical Association, 1977.

C.E. Carlston, *The Parables of the Triple Tradition.* Philadelphia. PA: Fortress Press, 1975.

C.H. Dodd, *The Parables of the Kingdom.* New York, NY: Charles Scribner's Sons, 1961.

J.R. Donahue, "Jesus as the Parable of God," *Interpretation* 32, (1978).

H.M. Humphrey, *A Bibliography for the Gospel of Mark, 1954–1980.* New York, NY — Toronto: Edwin Mellen Press, 1981.

N. Perrin, *Jesus and the Language of the Kingdom.* Philadelphia, PA: Fortress Press, 1976.

STUDY SESSION THREE

W.H. Kelber, *The Kingdom in Mark.* Philadelphia, PA: Fortress Press, 1974.

F. Kermode, *The Genesis of Secrecy.* Cambridge, MA: Harvard University Press, 1979.

Q. Quesnell, *The Mind of Mark.* Rome: Biblical Institute Press, 1969.

R.C. Tannehill, "The Disciples in Mark: The Function of a Narrative Role," *Journal of Religion 57,* (1977).

A. Weiser, *The Miracles of Jesus Then and Now.* Chicago, IL: Franciscan Herald, 1972.

STUDY SESSION FOUR

J.L. Blevins, *The Messianic Secret in Markan Research 1901–1976.* Washington, DC: University Press of America, 1981.

N. Perrin, *A Modern Pilgrimage in New Testament Christology.* Philadelphia, PA: Fortress Press, 1974.

L. Schenke, *Glory and the Way of the Cross.* Chicago, IL: Franciscan Herald, 1972.

W. Wrede, *The Messianic Secret.* Greenwood, SC: Attic Press, 1971.

STUDY SESSION FIVE

H.C. Kee, *Community of the New Age.* Philadelphia, PA: Westminster Press, 1977.

W.R. Telford, *The Barren Temple and the Withered Tree.* Sheffield, England: JSOT Press, 1980.

T.J. Weeden, *Mark — Transitions in Conflict.* Philadelphia, PA: Fortress Press, 1971.

STUDY SESSION SIX

J.R. Donahue, *Are You the Christ? The Trial Narrative in the Gospel of Mark.* Chico, CA: Scholars Press, 1973.

R.H. Fuller, *The Formation of the Resurrection Narratives.* Philadelphia, PA: Fortress Press, 1980.

D. Juel, *Messiah and Temple.* Chico, CA: Scholars Press, 1977.

W.H. Kelber (ed.), *The Passion in Mark.* Philadelphia, PA: Fortress Press, 1976.

G. O'Collins, *What Are They Saying About the Resurrection?* New York, NY — Ramsey, NJ — Toronto: Paulist, 1978.